Biography of Capote, Truman (1924-1984)

Truman Capote was born Truman Steckfus Persons in New Orleans on September 30, 1924 to 17-year-old Lillie Mae Faulk and Archulus ("Arch") Persons, a dissolute salesman. Capote's early life was marked by instability and poverty. When Faulk and Persons separated in 1928, he was left to be raised by relatives in Monroeville, Alabama, where he began what would become a lifelong friendship with Harper Lee, later the author of the renowned novel *To Kill A Mockingbird*. An unusual and observant child, Truman was determined to become a writer. He taught himself to read at age four and by age eight was "practicing" at writing in daily sessions. The details of the rural South, its oppressive poverty and wise, headstrong characters, impressed on the young Capote's imagination. He later drew on his memories of Alabama for some of his most famous writing.

In 1933, Lillie Mae, who then called herself Nina, remarried to a successful Cuban businessman, Joe Capote. Truman soon joined the couple in New York City, where he adopted his stepfather's surname and began an uneven career as a student in both private and public high schools in New York and Connecticut. While Capote was intelligent and highly focused on writing, he was uninterested in academics, and dropped out of his fourth year of high school when offered a 2-year contract position as a copy boy at the *New Yorker*. There, he attracted the attention of many of the city's literary and social elite, as much for his flamboyant wardrobe as for his mature, evocative prose. In 1942, Capote published his first short story, "Miriam", in the magazine *Mademoiselle*, which won him the 1946 prestigious O. Henry award for Best First-Published Story. He soon gained a contract with Random House, who advanced him $1500 for his first novel.

Other Voices, Other Rooms, published in 1948, was widely publicized, largely for Harold Halma's provocative back-cover author photo, which captured Capote lounging seductively on a chaise. The controversy surrounding the photo led to a storm of interest in the young novelist, and *Other Voices, Other Rooms* remained on the New York Times best-seller list for nine weeks. With his first novel, Capote became famous as a novelist and as a controversial figure who had captured the public's imagination. Capitalizing on Capote's sudden celebrity, Random House featured the Halma photo in their ads for the novel, which appeared in bookstore windows and continued to generate controversy.

Capote, now a celebrated member of New York's literary and social elite, followed the success of *Other Voices, Other Rooms* in 1949 with the acclaimed volume of short fiction, "A Tree of Night and Other Stories". In 1951, Random House published his novella, *The Grass Harp*, which he adapted as a play the following year. "Breakfast at Tiffany's: A Short Novel and Three Stories" was published alongside the serialization of "Breakfast at Tiffany's" in *Esquire* magazine, and proved so popular that the title story was quickly adapted for a major Hollywood film. With the publication of *In Cold Blood* in 1966, Capote secured his reputation as

one of the most important American writers of the century. A novel-length exploration of the aftermath of the real-life murder of a family in remote Holcomb, Kansas, *In Cold Blood* required extensive on-site research, and he took over five years to complete the manuscript. Serialized in the *New Yorker* in 1965 and published in hardcover by Random House the following year, *In Cold Blood* was an international best-seller and pioneered a new genre of literature: the non-fiction novel. Fragments from his final work, the unfinished novel *Answered Prayers*, were published as short stories in *Esquire* in 1975 and 1976, where they alienated the majority of Capote's celebrity friends, who recognized themselves as thinly-disguised characters in the work.

Capote's works are generally divided into three chronological periods. His early works are inconsistently styled with a focus on rural setting, family secrets and tragedy, and fall into the established genre of "Southern Gothic" fiction. *Other Voices, Other Rooms* and *The Grass Harp* belong to this early period. "Breakfast at Tiffany's" and its accompanying short stories, "House of Flowers", "A Diamond Guitar", and "A Christmas Memory" define Capote's middle period, which is characterized by a distinctively spare, direct prose style; minimal, linear plotlines, and a thematic obsession with eccentricity and the diversity of human love. This period also marks the development of what critics often call the "Capote narrator", the author's distinctive narrative persona who, while periodically participating in plotlines, remains conspicuously "objective", external to the story's narrative and emotional focus. The "Capote narrator" is also a distinguishing feature of *In Cold Blood* and the unfinished *An Answered Prayer*, the works of Capote's third period, which saw him moving towards his own, innovative hybrid of non-fiction and literary prose.

In his time in the public spotlight, Capote was renowned for his social stature and for his contributions to literature. His friends included actors, authors, critics, royalty, and aristocrats, whom he entertained in famous style. In 1966, in honor of Washington Post publisher Katharine Graham, Capote hosted the "Black & White Ball", a themed costume party widely regarded as the most important social event of the decade.

An open homosexual in a time when gays and lesbians were widely considered "deviant" or even criminal, Capote enjoyed an intimate, non-exclusive relationship with author Jack Dunphy from their first meeting in 1948 to Capote's death from liver failure in California on August 24, 1984. Today, Capote's life and works continue to capture public interest, with film versions of *Other Voices, Other Rooms*, *In Cold Blood*, and *The Grass Harp* released after his death. In 2005, the biographical film *Capote*, which dramatized the author's often difficult process of researching *In Cold Blood*, was nominated for numerous awards, and secured a Best Actor Academy Award for actor Phillip Seymour Hoffman's nuanced portrayal of the writer's struggle to maintain professional integrity in the face of his growing affection for the subjects of his work.

IN COLD BLOOD

Truman Capote

AUTHORED by Grace Laubacher
UPDATED AND REVISED by Damien Chazelle

COVER DESIGN by Table XI Partners LLC
COVER PHOTO by Olivia Verma and © 2005 GradeSaver, LLC

BOOK DESIGN by Table XI Partners LLC

Copyright © 2012 GradeSaver LLC

All rights reserved. No part of this publication may be reproduced, transmitted, or distributed in any form or by any means, electronic or mechanical, including photocopy, recording, any file sharing system, or any information storage and retrieval system, without the prior written permission of GradeSaver LLC.

Published by GradeSaver LLC, www.gradesaver.com

First published in the United States of America by GradeSaver LLC. 2009

GRADESAVER, the GradeSaver logo and the phrase "Getting you the grade since 1999" are registered trademarks of GradeSaver, LLC

ISBN 978-1-60259-186-8

Printed in the United States of America

For other products and additional information please visit
http://www.gradesaver.com

Table of Contents

Table of Contents

About In Cold Blood

In Cold Blood, which was published serially in The New Yorker in 1965 before appearing in book form in 1966, is the work that launched Truman Capote to literary stardom, and remains his best-known piece. It details the events of a real-life murder case that took place in Finney County, in western Kansas, between 1959 and 1965. On the night of November 14th, 1959, two men entered a home in Holcomb, Kansas, and slaughtered four members of the Clutter family, a wealthy and respected household in Finney County. The apparent randomness and unfounded brutality of the act, the likes of which had rarely been seen in this part of Kansas, shocked and disturbed the surrounding community, as its residents saw their peaceful and anonymous lifestyle suddenly invaded by law enforcement, the media, and the watchful eyes of the rest of the nation.

Among those keenly interested in the case was Truman Capote. Flipping through The New York Times on a November morning, he had come across a brief article outlining the murders with only the barest details ("Wealthy Farmer, 3 of Family Slain"), and imagined the case could be the subject of his next project, a long-form work of nonfiction. By mid-December, he was on a train to Kansas, eager to see what more he could uncover.

The investigation went on for six weeks, during which time Capote attempted to earn the favor and cooperation of Holcomb's residents and interview them about their experiences. He was accompanied by his childhood friend, Nelle Harper Lee, author of To Kill a Mockingbird. She, well acquainted with the ways of small-town rural life, gained the confidence of Holcomb's residents far more quickly than Capote, whose flamboyant demeanor quickly set him apart from many of his subjects and rendered him somewhat of an outsider. Just before the first real break in the murder case, however, Capote got a break of his own: he and Lee were invited to the home of Clifford Hope, a lawyer in Garden City, for Christmas dinner, and the Hopes, much to their surprise, were quite charmed by him. Before long, Capote became a kind of curiosity in Garden City and Holcomb, and those involved in the case gradually opened their homes and their hearts to him.

Shortly before New Year's, 1960, the perpetrators – identified as Richard "Dick" Hickock and Perry Edward Smith – were apprehended in Las Vegas and transferred to Finney County, where they were tried and convicted of the killings. They spent five years on Death Row, during which time they corresponded regularly with Capote and provided him with numerous interviews, as well as written accounts of their personal histories and experiences. Capote developed a particular affection for Perry Smith, the scrawnier and more sensitive of the two, who had allegedly pulled the trigger on all four victims. Smith was highly intelligent and creative, yet scarred from a turbulent upbringing by neglectful parents – much like Capote himself. Their relationship was such that, as Harper Lee put it, "Each looked at the other and saw – or thought he saw – the man he might have been." A number of critics and eyewitnesses have suggested that their relationship may have been romantic, and it may have been, but it is also possible that they merely shared a sensibility shaped by common experiences.

After a number of appeals and postponements, the prisoners were hanged in the early hours of the morning on April 14, 1965. Capote, ambivalent to the end about the execution – on the one hand, he needed an ending to complete his book, but on the other, he had become incredibly emotionally tied to the prisoners – was present at the execution. Despondent yet relieved, he finished the last installment of the book in June of 1965, and it was set for publication that fall.

In Cold Blood is considered an example of "New Journalism," a genre that was pioneered in the 1960s and 70s by Capote as well as Tom Wolfe, Norman Mailer, Hunter S. Thompson, and Joan Didion, among others. (Capote, however, disliked this branding, referring instead to his work as a "nonfiction novel.") The New Journalists were the first to employ literary techniques – or techniques adapted from fiction writing – to present their nonfiction narratives. The result was a new brand of in-depth, novelistic coverage of real-world events, presented from the perspective of individuals experiencing them firsthand (including the writer him/herself, who carried out extensive field research in order to capture the complete picture of events).

The much-anticipated first section of In Cold Blood appeared in The New Yorker in September of 1965, breaking the magazine's sales record. The four installments garnered the highest praise from critics and readers alike, who commended their "Homeric" storytelling and the depth of Capote's characterization, especially of Dick and Perry. When the book was finally published in full by Random House in early 1966, his new "masterpiece" rocketed Capote to celebrity status, and ranked him among the literary giants of his era. In Cold Blood remains one of the most significant works of literature of the twentieth century, both for its merging of journalistic and literary storytelling, and for its unprecedented insight into the nature of criminality in American culture.

Character List

Herb Clutter

The prominent and respected owner and proprietor of River Valley Farm, Herb is the patriarch of the Clutter family, husband to Bonnie Clutter and father to four children: Eveanna, Beverly, Nancy and Kenyon. He is a generous employer, and an active churchgoer and "die-hard community booster" (21). He runs a disciplined household, and keeps himself to a strict day-to-day regimen. Ultimately, however, his righteous and well-to-do lifestyle plays him into the hands of his killers, who make him first the target of their attempted robbery and, later, a scapegoat for their own resentments.

Bonnie Clutter

Herb's wife and mother to Nancy and Kenyon, Bonnie is a slight, nervous, apologetic woman who suffers from chronic postpartum depression, which leaves her bedridden on many days. Having lived a sheltered childhood, she gave up her training as a nurse to marry Herb and settle into her responsibilities as a housewife. Her depression has gradually isolated her from many of her close friends, and she spends her last afternoon locked away in her room, regretting her inability to socialize or be a stronger mother to her children.

Nancy Clutter

Nancy, who is sixteen years old, is a model student, the president of her class, and a leader in a number of community activities, including the Young Methodists League and the local 4-H club. She also devotes time to teaching younger girls music, sewing, and baking; in fact, her only shortcoming seems to be her tendency to over-commit herself to helping others. She is dating – and claims to be in love with – Bobby Rupp, the star of the high school basketball team. This is a point of contention between Nancy and her father, who wishes she would break off the relationship, since Bobby is Catholic, and the Clutters are Methodist. Nancy spends her last day baking a cherry pie with her young neighbor, instructing another girl in music, and caring for her horse, Babe. During the attempted robbery, prior to her murder, she manages the situation by chatting with the intruders in a cool and friendly fashion; Perry later claims to have liked her, in spite of what he later does to her.

Kenyon Clutter

Kenyon, who is fifteen, is more solitary than his sister, and uninterested in dating, preferring to spend his time in the Clutters' basement workshop, where he does carpentry and mechanical projects. He also hunts rabbits, and spends time in his pickup truck with his best friend Bob Jones.

Perry Smith

Perry is responsible for the deaths of all four members of the Clutter family. Although he originally resists even the idea of the robbery, the charged atmosphere of the Clutter home prompts him to a frenzy of frustration and resentment, and the Clutters become the unfortunate targets of his fury. Prior to this revelation, however, we learn that he is sensitive, thoughtful, creative, and highly intelligent. He comes from a troubled background, and he harbors escapist fantasies of grand adventures in exotic locales, and of being rescued from his woes by beautiful yellow parrots. His demure, reflective presence is a sharp contrast to Dick's bombastic personality, and the pair spend much of their time at friendly odds with one another.

Dick Hickock

Dick initiates the plan to rob the Clutters, but wavers when the time comes to carry out the murders, and instead becomes a bystander as Perry executes all four members of the family. Dick is a self-assured, smooth-talking petty criminal, who is always scheming to make a quick buck, but at times his bluster outstrips his real commitment to the plans he initiates. According to Perry, Dick is a "real masculine type," a charismatic and commanding individual whom Perry feels compelled to "stick by," in spite of his disapproval of some of Dick's behaviors. By the end of the book, however, we become aware of some of Dick's own insecurities: his failure to achieve financial security and support his first wife, Carol, and their three children, and his sexual interest in young girls, both of which he compensates for with bravado and reckless criminal actions.

Alvin Dewey

Dewey is the lead investigator on the Clutter case, and, as a former friend of Herb and Bonnie, he develops an obsessive interest in tracking down the perpetrators, sacrificing his physical and mental health for the six weeks they are at large. He lives in Garden City with his wife and two sons, and through Dewey we experience the many of the mixed emotions circulating in the town pertaining to the search, arrest, and trial of the two killers.

Susan Kidwell

Susan (or "Sue") Kidwell is Nancy's closest friend and confidante, and is one of two girls to discover the murders on the morning of November 15th. Throughout the novel, she reflects fondly on her friendship with Nancy and her childhood memories at the Clutters', becoming a symbol of graceful and forgiving resilience in the wake of unspeakable tragedy.

Bobby Rupp

Bobby Rupp is Nancy's boyfriend, and the star of the high school basketball team. Immediately following the discovery of the murders, he is singled out as a suspect, adding personal indignity to the devastating loss of Nancy and her family.

Tex John Smith

Perry's father, a former rodeo rider who now resides in Alaska. Perry has mixed emotions when it comes to his father, but mainly he resents Tex John for holding him back as an adolescent.

Barbara Johnson

Perry's sister, with whom he has a troubled relationship. She lives in San Fransisco with her husband and three children, and she and Perry rarely communicate.

Walter Hickock

Dick's father, who lives in Olathe with his wife, Eunice and the Hickocks' younger son.

Eunice Hickcock

Dick's mother.

Floyd Wells

Dick's cellmate at the Kansas State Penitentiary, and a former employee at River Valley Farm, who told Dick that Herb Clutter kept ten thousand dollars in a safe in his house. Wells is the one to tip off the detectives about Perry and Dick, which eventually results in their arrest.

Clarence Duntz

A detective at the Kansas Bureau of Investigation, part of the four-person team who tracks down the killers.

Roy Church

Another K.B.I. detective, also a member of the team.

Harold Nye

Another K.B.I. detective, also a member of the team.

Nancy Ewalt

A friend of Nancy Clutter's who, along with Susan Kidwell, discovers the murders on the morning of November 15th.

Earl Robinson

The sheriff of Finney county.

Willie-Jay

Perry's pious and philosophic friend from the Kansas State Penitentiary, who called him "exceptional." Perry considers Willie-Jay to be his "real and only friend."

Reverend James Post

The Protestant chaplain in Lansing, where Perry was formerly imprisoned. While under Willie-Jay's tutelage, Perry painted a portrait of Jesus which the Reverend now keeps in his office, as a testament to Perry's character.

Paul Helm

The groundskeeper at River Valley Farm.

Marie Dewey

Alvin's wife.

Eveanna Jarchow

The eldest daughter of Herb and Bonnie Clutter, who is married and lives in northern Illinois.

Beverly Clutter (later, Beverly English)

The Clutters' second daughter, who is studying to be a nurse in Kansas City.

Bob Johnson

The insurance agent who sells Herb Clutter his life insurance policy.

Mrs. Ashida

A resident of Holcomb for two years, whom Herb Clutter has elected to honor at the 4-H Achievement Banquet. After the murders, she and her husband Hideo decide to move out of state.

Bess Hartman

Owner of Hartman's Café, a local eatery (and rumor mill) in Holcomb.

Myrtle Clare

The Holcomb postmistress.

Sadie ("Mother") Truitt

The Holcomb mail messenger, and Myrtle Clare's mother.

Mr. Bell

A motorist whom Perry and Dick almost murder and rob near Omaha, but they are thwarted at the last minute when Bell pulls over for another hitchhiker.

Bill

A boy who hitches a ride with Perry and Dick in Texas, along with his grandfather, and teaches them to hunt for discarded bottles to redeem for cash.

Johnny

Bill's grandfather

Wendle Meier

The Finney county undersheriff, who resides next to Perry's cell in the Garden City jailhouse.

Josephine Meier

Wendle's wife, who cooks for Perry and tries to make him as comfortable as possible.

Arthur Fleming

Perry's state-appointed defense attorney.

Harrison Smith

Dick's state-appointed defense attorney.

Don Cullivan

A friend from Perry's army days who testifies as a "character witness" for Perry. While in Garden City, Don dines with Perry and attempts to comfort him by telling him about God's love and mercy (Perry is unconvinced).

Roland Tate

The judge in the Clutter murder trial.

Logan Green

The prosecutor in the Clutter trial.

Dr. W. Mitchell Jones

A specialist in criminal psychology from the Larned State Hospital, who examines Perry and Dick in preparation for the trial. He prepares a comprehensive diagnosis of the two defendants, but is prevented from testifying in court.

Dr. Joseph Satten

A contemporary of Dr. Jones, who publishes an article with findings that resemble Dr. Jones' conclusions about Perry, indicating that Perry's psychosis is not an isolated or unique phenomenon.

Lowell Lee Andrews

Another prisoner on death row, who has been convicted of the cold-blooded murders of his parents and sister. Andrews, like Perry, suffers from a probable case of schizophrenia, but his plea of insanity is also shot down by the M'Naghten rule.

Ronnie York / James Latham

Two teenagers who join the row in 1961, having been convicted of a cross-country murder spree.

Major Themes

Modern-day Mythology/Epic Storytelling

In Cold Blood is crafted like a modern-day tragedy, on the scale of one of the Greek dramas from classical antiquity, and deals with many of the same universal themes: murder, vengeance, and the pursuit of justice. This, for Capote, was the power of his new literary genre, the nonfiction novel: to take events from the contemporary world and elevate them to epic storytelling proportions, enabling them to transcend their specific historical moment and reflect on broader truths about humanity. Capote assembles the disparate facts and perspectives about the Clutter case into a narrative that speaks profoundly on the nature of human life and death, criminality, American society and the pursuit of individual happiness -- reinventing in the process many of our modern-day forms of mythology (for example, the myth of the American dream).

Loss of Innocence/Undermining the American Dream

The Clutter killings are a turning point for the citizens of Holcomb and Garden City: for the first time, the dangerous wider world seems to threaten their peaceful existence, and their former naïveté gives way to feelings of doubt, fear and suspicion. According to Capote, it is the first time the citizens of this part of Kansas have had to endure the "unique experience of distrusting each other" (88). Their version of the American dream – of safety, security, and the ability to determine their own fate – becomes undermined, if not entirely thwarted, by the victimization of the Clutters. Their view of the world must suddenly include another kind of person, a poor, embittered, "rootless" person, for whom this dream was never an option in the first place.

The Banality of Evil

When the murders are first discovered, Perry and Dick, as "persons unknown," are elevated to an inhuman, almost mythic stature, the essence of a pure and motiveless evil that has come to destroy the peaceful lifestyle of the Holcomb residents. Capote, however, replaces this simplistic view with a more nuanced and sensitive interpretation, by exploring the material, psychological, environmental circumstances that cause two otherwise ordinary human beings to commit such an atrocious act. Throughout the novel, Perry and Dick are transformed from heartless, cold-blooded menaces, whose actions seem to defy human logic, into the fraught, pitiful, completely humanized individuals they are at the end of the book, and the crime itself is boiled down to a very basic and fairly understandable set of emotional responses. Although he does not attempt to excuse their actions, Capote shows how ordinary feelings of frustration and despair accidentally erupt into such an extraordinary crime. The book seems to contend that criminality and "evil" are not things apart, as we tend to define them, but normal human responses that merely become amplified and find a destructive outlet.

Family

Family life is a key determinant of individual character in the context of the book. The Clutters, who symbolize the utmost integrity of family life, are obliterated by Perry, who represents everything it means to come from a broken home. The Clutters' uprightness is related to the strength of their family, as Perry's criminality is connected to the dissolution of his own kinship ties. In spirit, Dick is still wedded to his first wife, and his dreams of becoming self-sufficient are linked to the ability to support her and their three sons. The strength of a person's family ties has the larger implication of whether that person can live happily, well-off, and in a self-determined fashion. (The exception to this rule is with regard to Dick's parents, who seem to have raised him lovingly and for whom he has genuine respect and affection, despite his criminal tendencies.)

Socioeconomic Status

The Clutter killings are symbolic of a class conflict, highlighting the discrepancy between the affluent, middle-class, predominantly white citizens of Holcomb and the underprivileged, working-class, mixed-race (in the case of Perry) killers. Theft is the only form of economic mobility that Perry and Dick have ever known, as neither of them have had a chance at a proper education or a solid career (Dick, we learn, could not afford to attend college, and Perry was forced to help his father earn their basic subsistence in Alaska). Economic insecurity is at the root of the murders on every level: it forms the initial motive for the break-in (to steal the contents of Herb Clutter's safe), and later on causes Perry to feel ashamed, for "crawling on my belly to steal a child's silver dollar" (240), a sentiment which is ultimately to blame for the fatal turn the robbery takes.

Self-Image

The theme of self- or ego-image is crucial to understanding the interpersonal dynamics of Perry and Dick, especially those that lead to the eventual murder spree. Both men, Perry especially, are highly image-conscious and attuned to how others perceive them. Towards the end of the book, we learn from Perry's psychiatric evaluation that he is "overly sensitive to criticisms that others make of him, and cannot tolerate being made fun of. He is quick to sense slight or insult in things others say" (297). In some sense, the rivalry between Dick and Perry is a mutual struggle for self-recognition, with each wishing the other man would validate his own self-image (this may be fueled, as some critics have suggested, by homoerotic desire). Self-image represents, in a larger sense, social status and self-determination, neither of which is available to these men. For Perry, the botched robbery at the Clutters is a painful reminder of his own lack of means or social mobility, and his feelings of shame and self-loathing at this realization are ultimately at the root of his homicidal rampage.

Homosexuality

Homoerotic desire is just below the surface of the relationship between Dick and Perry, between Perry and Willie-Jay, and, more implicitly, in the meta-textual relationship of Truman Capote to his two subjects. Whether or not these attractions were overtly acknowledged or even consciously realized by their subjects (Capote thought it was likely that both men had repressed these feelings), they are a palpable subtext of the narrative and serve several functions. On one level, they elucidate the relationship of Dick and Perry, adding a layer of intensity to their interactions that helps to explain why, for example, they might have become so frustrated at the Clutter home, or why so much of Perry's self-image rests on Dick's opinion of him. But the theme of homosexuality also functions as a larger symbol of, and premise for, Dick and Perry's status as outsiders, social misfits for whom conventional society seems to have no place. At the time that In Cold Blood was penned, homosexuals were considered a threat to the social order, so much so that the F.B.I. kept official watch lists in order to monitor their activities. This unspoken element of their relationship heightens the intensity of their clash with conservative, small-town American life, and raises the stakes of the murder trial by a perceptible margin.

Mental Illness

Perry and Dick's criminal tendencies are revealed to have underlying medical causes (Perry suffers from paranoid schizophrenia, and Dick has brain damage from a concussion); the difficulty of the murder trial becomes, to what extent are they still accountable for their actions? In a larger sense, the book seems to grapple with the question of whether the same moral standards are applicable to all people, regardless of their upbringing and their life circumstances; or whether Perry and Dick are in some measure redeemed (at least morally, if not legally) by the fact of their mental illness, and the fact that their own lives have been so lacking.

Glossary of Terms

4-H

A youth development program administered through the United States Department of Agriculture. Although it was originally geared toward instructing American youth in agricultural skills and technology, its mission also includes teaching leadership and general life skills, particularly to children in rural areas.

aft

The back of a boat (the stern)

agoraphobia

Fear of public and/or unfamiliar places. Individuals who suffer from agoraphobia are often afraid to leave the vicinity of their home.

cavalcade

A procession of cars or sometimes, riders on horseback

contrition

Repentance; the act of asking for forgiveness

emporium

A retail store, often carrying many different forms of merchandise; a place of trade

fleece

To defraud; or deprive of money through trickery

Foxtrot

A ballroom dance that became popular in the early part of the twentieth century; it was originally accompanied by ragtime music, which gradually became replaced by swing.

gemütlich

From German: greeably pleasant

Heathcliff

A character from Emily Brontë's *Wuthering Heights*; the name connotes an archetypal romantic hero

hoofer

A professional dancer

ineffable

Inexpressible, impossible to capture in words

Lilliputian

Very small (a reference to the undersized residents of Lilliput in Gulliver's Travels)

mélange

From French: a medley or mixture of incongruous elements

mica

A mineral known for its distinct shine, which is often used for decorative purposes

Old Grad

A former prison inmate; an ex-convict

pedophiliac

A person who takes a sexual interest in children.

pragmatic

Oriented towards practical matters, as opposed to intellectual or artistic ones.

precipitate

To hasten the arrival of, or bring about

rankle

To cause irritation or resentment; to fester

slug

A fake coin

touristic

Pertaining to tourism

Vaudeville

A genre of theatrical entertainment, popular in the United States in the late nineteenth and early twentieth centuries, consisting of a number of separate, unrelated acts.

venire

An entire panel from which a jury is drawn.

Glossary of Terms

virile

Masculine; pertaining to manhood

voir dire

A preliminary examination to determine the competency of a witness or juror

Glossary of Terms

Short Summary

The Clutter family – Herbert and Bonnie, and their teenage children, Nancy and Kenyon – lead a prosperous and principled life on their farm in Holcomb, a small rural settlement in western Kansas. They are prominent and respected members of the community, in both Holcomb and the neighboring Garden City, and Herb Clutter is known to be a generous employer. Their life is disciplined, but pleasant and well provided for. The narration follows the Clutters through the events of November 14th, 1959, which is ominously referred to as the family's "last." In another part of Kansas, two men on parole from the Kansas State Penitentiary, Dick Hickock and Perry Smith, are planning a "score," which includes a 12-gauge shotgun, rubber gloves, rope, and black stockings. Over the course of the day, they make their way in the direction of Garden City by car, making various stops along the way. They arrive shortly after midnight, and proceed to the Clutter farm.

On the morning of November 15th, two friends of Nancy Clutter's arrive at the house and find Nancy upstairs, dead from a shotgun blast to the head. The authorities, in turn, find three more bodies: all four Clutters have been brutally murdered, the children and Bonnie with a shotgun, and Herb Clutter with a knife to the throat. The police find very little evidence at the crime scene: only two sets of boot prints, and the materials used to bind the victims. The residents of Garden City and Holcomb are shocked and deeply troubled by the murders, and many speculate that the killer or killers may be among them.

An investigation is launched, led by Alvin Dewey. The team also includes Special Agents Clarence Duntz, Harold Nye, and Roy Church. Perry and Dick are already far away in Kansas City, reading about the crime in the newspaper and wondering about the likelihood that it will be traced to them. While the detectives begin their search for physical evidence and witness testimonials, the fugitives head for Mexico, pausing only long enough to earn some quick cash by dropping bad checks in Kansas City.

Details about the murderers are slowly revealed in the course of the narration. Perry dreams of grand adventures and of being whisked away from his troubles by beautiful parrots; his escapist reveries are a way of compensating for the trauma of his childhood and his degraded lifestyle. He is self-conscious, sensitive, and philosophic. Dick, on the other hand, is cocky, self-assured, and pragmatic; financial irresponsibility has led him away from a solid upbringing to a life of petty crime. His ambitions are also a way of compensating for his lack of means, but his bluster and bravado stand in sharp contrast to Perry's demure presence.

The investigative team receives its first lead in the form of Floyd Wells, a former employee of Herb Clutter's who celled with Dick at the Kansas State Penitentiary, and who told Dick that the Clutters kept a locked safe full of cash in their home. The detectives follow up on Wells' testimony, and discover that both Dick and Perry were traveling on the night of the killings. Meanwhile, the fugitives have returned to the United States, and continue to roam the countryside, hitchhiking. Eventually, the police trace a stolen car to them, and they are apprehended in Las Vegas just before New Years', six weeks after the murders.

During the interrogation, the detectives only gradually reveal that the two men are wanted for quadruple homicide. Catching Dick in a web of lies and false alibis, they succeed in forcing a confession out of him, but he blames Perry for all four murders. En route to Garden City, Agent Dewey convinces Perry, in turn, that Dick has confessed to the crime, and Perry, finally defeated, provides a lengthy account of how the murders transpired. According to Perry, their initial aim was to rob the Clutters, having heard from Floyd Wells that Herb Clutter kept ten thousand dollars in a safe inside the house. When they arrived and found no safe, nor anything else of significant value, Perry had wanted to abandon the scene, but Dick urged him to stay and follow through: "No witnesses." Trying to make Dick admit that he couldn't actually go through with the killings, Perry himself took up the knife, meaning "to call his bluff," but was seized by sudden emotion, and to his surprise found himself slitting Mr. Clutter's throat. The subsequent shootings all happened in a blind frenzy on the part of the killers, after which they fled the scene.

The men are put on trial in Garden City. In the course of the trial, the prisoners undergo a psychiatric evaluation, during which it is concluded that both show definite signs of mental illness and emotional dysfunction. Perry almost certainly suffers from paranoid schizophrenia, and Dick has brain damage incurred in a car accident as a young man. In the case of Perry, who has confessed to all four murders, the doctors conclude that the killings functioned as a form of unconscious retribution for all the misfortunes and disappointments of his life, beginning in his childhood. For Perry, the Clutters and their immaculate lifestyle symbolized everything the world had denied him, and their murders, beginning with Herb Clutter, were a quasi-automatic response.

In spite of these findings, the court upholds the M'Naghten rule, which disregards mental illness in determining whether criminals are responsible for their actions. Dick and Perry are found guilty of four counts of murder in the first degree, and sentenced to death by hanging. They spend five years on Death Row, where they are joined by Lowell Lee Andrews, Ronnie York and James Latham, all high-profile murderers. In spite of numerous appeals, as well as allegations of mistrial (from Dick), they are hanged on April 14th, 1965, before a crowd of twenty witnesses.

The last scene belongs to Alvin Dewey, who visits the cemetery where the Clutters are buried, and marvels at the persistence of life, even in the aftermath of such hopeless tragedy.

Quotes and Analysis

"The village of Holcomb stands on the high wheat plains of western Kansas, a lonesome area that other Kansans call 'out there.' . . .The land is flat, the views are awesomely extensive; horses, herds of cattle, a white cluster of grain elevators rising as gracefully as Greek temples are visible long before a traveler reaches them."

pg. 3

The book begins and ends with descriptions of the landscape; the serenity of the plains is an unlikely setting for a tragedy, which makes it all the more disturbing when one does occur. The book starts by taking the "long view" of its subjects, outlining them from a distance before eventually zooming in to probe the microscopic details of the case, a trajectory that reflects Capote's own dealings with the residents of Holcomb and Garden City. Here, also, Capote compares the landscape to that of ancient Greece, indicating that the story contained in these pages has larger significance as an examination of timeless human themes.

"This hitherto peaceful congregation of neighbors and old friends had suddenly to endure the unique experience of distrusting each other; understandably, they believed that the murderer was among themselves."

pg. 88

The Clutter killings wreak havoc on the security of Holcomb, fragmenting the community and sowing the first seeds of doubt and suspicion. In allegorical terms, the residents of Holcomb experience a kind of fall from grace, and a loss of their former innocence, as for the first time they are forced to confront the unseemly reality of the killers and the world they represent.

"'Deal me out, baby,' Dick said. 'I'm a normal.' And Dick meant what he said. He thought of himself as balanced, as sane as anyone—maybe a bit smarter than the average fellow, that's all. But Perry—there was, in Dick's opinion, 'something wrong' with Little Perry."

pg. 108

Dick uses Perry as a foil for his own self-image, often belittling or impugning him for his more eccentric, "childish," or effeminate qualities, in comparison with which Dick convinces himself that he is "normal." Perry, on the other hand, prides himself on being "exceptional," sensitive, even "artistic" in comparison to Dick. However, each man looks to the other for affirmation of his own masculinity, Dick latching onto Perry for his "killer instincts," and Perry yearning for Dick to think him "hard, as much the 'masculine type' as he considered Dick to be" (111).

"No, sir, I wouldn't have him in the house. One look and I saw what he was. With his perfume. And his oily hair. It was clear as day where Dick had met him."

Mrs. Hickock, pg. 169

Mrs. Hickock makes a snap judgment of Perry, based on his appearance, which alienates him from their household, and at the same time speaks more generally to how Perry is perceived in the eyes of "conventional" Americans. Whether or not his "perfume" and "oily hair" are signifiers of a homosexual orientation - as Mrs. Hickock presumes - they mark Perry as different and, symbolically, divorced from the family-oriented, middle-class American values that other characters so preciously uphold.

"They shared a doom against which virtue was no defense."

Barbara, reflecting on herself and Perry, pg. 185

In a moment of despair, Barbara takes a deterministic view of her and Perry's lives. Wishing to rid herself of the burden of their troubled upbringing, she has settled into a comfortable and secure life with her husband; but Perry is a constant reminder of her past, and his run-ins with the law feed her own insecurities that she, too, will one day succumb to the fate of her siblings and parents. Unnerved by this possibility, she turns her back on Perry, causing him to venture further down the path of self-destruction and isolation.

"[Dick] was holding the knife. I asked him for it, and he gave it to me, and I said, 'All right, Dick. Here goes.' But I didn't mean it. I meant to call his bluff, make him argue me out of it, make him admit he was a phony and a coward. See, it was something between me and Dick. I knelt down beside Mr. Clutter, and the pain of kneeling—I thought of that goddam dollar. Silver dollar. The shame. Disgust. And they'd told me never to come back to Kansas. But I didn't realize what I'd done till I heard the sound. Like somebody drowning. Screaming under water."

Perry, pg. 244

Perry describes his motivation for the first of the killings. It begins with a rivalrous confrontation with Dick over whether Dick will go through with his promise to "blast hair all over the walls"; this is quickly eclipsed by Perry's feelings of shame and self-loathing while reflecting on the indignity of the botched robbery and, by association, the indignity of his life as a criminal. He is hardly conscious of slitting Herb Clutter's throat; the murder comes as a kind of automatic response to the memory of other frustrations and insults he has endured, of which the Clutter household is symbolic.

"I didn't want to harm the man. I thought he was a very nice gentleman. Soft-spoken. I thought so right up to the moment I cut his throat."

Perry, pg. 244

Perry claims to have liked Mr. Clutter, as well as the other members of the family; this at first seems ironic, but in fact it says a great deal about Perry's motive for killing the Clutters. The murders, it seems, were not inspired by a literal hatred of this specific family, but by misdirected frustration and resentment that finds a symbolic object in the Clutters and the values that they represent. The family is unlucky enough to be on the receiving end of this fury, but they are by no means its source.

"The crime was a psychological accident, virtually an impersonal act; the victims might as well have been killed by lightning. Except for one thing: they had experienced prolonged terror, they had suffered. And Dewey could not forget their sufferings. Nonetheless, he found it possible to look at the man beside him without anger—with, rather, a measure of sympathy—for Perry Smith's life had been no bed of roses but pitiful, an ugly and lonely progress toward one mirage or another."

pg. 245-246

Dewey is ambivalent about the moral implications of the Clutter case: while he acknowledges the detestable nature of the crimes, he finds it difficult to wholeheartedly condemn the men responsible, for they too have suffered in unspeakable ways, and beyond this, seem to have lost control of themselves in committing the murders. The Clutters represent everything that Perry has been denied in his own life; Dewey's sentiments are close to those of the book as a whole, which emphasizes the difficulty of making an absolute moral judgment of the killers one way or the other.

"When Smith attacked Mr. Clutter he was under a mental eclipse, deep inside a schizophrenic darkness."

pg. 302

This quote is from the clinical analysis of Perry's criminal tendencies, and it legitimizes Perry's claim that he was not in complete control of his actions when he carried out the murders of the Clutters. He was, rather, acting out of his medical incapacity to manage his emotional responses.

"Dewey was fifty-one, four years older than when he supervised the Clutter investigation. . . . The dream of settling on his farm had not come true, for his wife's fear of living in that sort of isolation had never lessened. Instead, the Deweys had built a new house in town; they were proud of it, and proud, too, of both their sons, who were deep-voiced now and as tall as their father. The older boy was headed for college in the autumn."

pg. 341

The book concludes from the perspective of Alvin Dewey, and the developments of his life since the Clutter case reflect the passage of time and the resilience of the surrounding community in the wake of the deaths. The memory of the Clutters persists, having made its permanent impression on their lives; but nonetheless, Dewey and his family are oriented towards the future, taking in stride the triumphs and the losses of the passing years.

Summary and Analysis of The Last to See Them Alive, Part 1 (pgs. 3-57)

The reader is introduced to the village of Holcomb, a small yet prosperous farming settlement in western Kansas. Herbert Clutter, a self-made man and prominent member of the community, lives a comfortable life as the owner and proprietor of River Valley Farm, where he resides with his wife, Bonnie, and children, Nancy (sixteen), and Kenyon (fifteen). The Clutters are a principled and upstanding family, active churchgoers and participants in community life, both in Holcomb and the neighboring Garden City.

Nancy, who is a "straight-A student, the president of her class, a leader in the 4-H program and the Young Methodists league, a skilled rider, an excellent musician, and an annual winner at the county fair," also volunteers her time to instruct younger girls in baking and other domestic occupations, and has recently played a principal role in the school production of "Tom Sawyer." Kenyon, more reticent than his sister, spends much of his time woodworking in the Clutters' basement shop, or hunting rabbits with his best friend Bob Jones. The Clutters' peaceful and contented existence is marred only by the fact that Bonnie Clutter suffers from clinical depression, a condition that leaves her bedridden on many days; however, doctors have finally traced her ailment to dislocation in her spinal column, and she is expected to make a full recovery.

The narration takes the reader through the events of Saturday, November 14th, which is ominously described as the family's "last." Nancy instructs a young neighbor, Jolene Katz, in the baking of a cherry pie. Kenyon puts the finishing touches on a hope chest he has built as a wedding present for his older sister, and then travels with his father to a meeting of the 4-H club in Garden City. Bonnie Clutter spends a typical afternoon in bed.

Four hundred miles away, in Olathe, Kansas, a man named Perry Smith awaits the arrival of his friend and compatriot, Richard "Dick" Hickock. Dick has planned a "score," for which he requires Perry's assistance. While he waits, Perry peruses a series of maps, dreaming of treasure-hunting expeditions in exotic locales, South America in particular. Upon Dick's arrival, we learn that both men are on parole from the Kansas State Penitentiary. The nature of the "score" is not yet made explicit, but Dick has stolen his father's twelve-gauge shotgun and has fabricated a story that the pair are planning to visit Perry's sister in Fort Scott. They take to the road, making various stops along the way to purchase supplies: rubber gloves, rope, black stockings.

Perry, thoughtful and reserved, reflects on his earliest encounters with Dick and the other inmates of the Kansas Penitentiary, including the pious and philosophic Willie-Jay, whom Perry regards as his "real and only friend." Willie-Jay's esteemed opinion of Perry as "exceptional" and "artistic" (45) is contrasted with Dick's impatience with his companion's sensitive and cautious outlook in their early interactions.

Back in Holcomb, Herb Clutter meets with a representative of New York Life Insurance, and takes out a forty-thousand-dollar policy, which pays double indemnity in the event of death by accidental means. Later that evening, the Clutters are visited by Bobby Rupp, Nancy's boyfriend. Herb Clutter disapproves of the relationship: while the Clutters are Methodist, the Rupps are Catholic, and for this reason he will not consider allowing Nancy to marry Bobby. Nonetheless, Herb is cordial to Bobby. Before retiring, Nancy reflects on the situation and records a few notes from the day in her five-year diary.

Perry and Dick stop for gas at a Phillip's 66 in Garden City at around midnight, before making their way to Holcomb and eventually, River Valley Farm.

Analysis:

Critics have described the opening passage of In Cold Blood as "Homeric" (after the Greek epic poet Homer, the author of the Iliad and Odyssey). Capote's descriptions of the landscape and built environment lend them a mythological stature, foreshadowing the enormity of the events to follow: "The land is flat, and the views are awesomely extensive; horses, herds of cattle, a white cluster of grain elevators rising as gracefully as the Greek temples are visible long before a traveler reaches them" (3). Finney County becomes the theatre of a tragedy about to unfold, whose proportions exceed the specific time and place in which they occur, allowing the book to become a kind of universal rumination on the nature of violence and the human spirit. Capote said that he chose his subject matter partly for its timeless appeal: "The human heart being what it is, murder was a theme not likely to darken or yellow with time." The references to classical antiquity, then, underscore the universality of Capote's engagement.

The Clutter lifestyle is unimpeachable, almost to a fault. If Herb Clutter is comparable to the hero in a Greek tragedy, then his self-righteous attitude is his hubris, the tragic flaw that results (indirectly) in his demise. He holds himself, his family, and his employees to the strictest standards: he does not tolerate alcohol, or even mild stimulants such as caffeine; he keeps his children on a short leash (Nancy is rarely allowed out of the house after ten); and he runs his ranch like clockwork. In exchange for this rigidity, however, he provides liberally for his family and employees, and has succeeded in turning River Valley Farm into a highly profitable enterprise. This enviable lifestyle makes him a likely target for Dick and Perry's scheme, and, as is revealed later in the book, plays a direct role in fueling the psychological rampage that results in the deaths of all four Clutters.

Capote introduces Perry with an ironic flourish, by comparing him to Herb: "Like Mr. Clutter, the young man breakfasting in a café called the Little Jewel never drank coffee" (14). Here the similarity ends, for Perry is in many ways the polar opposite of Herb Clutter. He is a romantic, dreaming of treasure-hunting adventures in far-flung locales; adventures which, based on what we know of him right now, are not supported by any realistic financial means. Perry and Dick are both physically maimed from motor-vehicle accidents, a detail that not only discloses the recklessness of their lifestyles, but also hints at subtler forms of emotional damage. While Herb Clutter celebrates the fact that he has been pronounced "in first-rate condition" in a recent medical examination, Perry nurses his aching knees in a gas station men's room.

We also begin to glimpse elements of the complex interpersonal dynamic of Perry and Dick. Dick is easygoing and self-assured, where Perry is cautious and reflective; Perry admires Dick for being a "real masculine type," but Dick needs Perry for what he considers to be Perry's "natural killer" tendencies (based on stories Perry has told him). Yet in spite of this mutual esteem for one another, the two men's relationship features elements of insecure rivalry, coupled with just enough disdain to keep the men at arm's length.

Significantly, we are told that Perry's original reason for returning to Kansas was to meet up with Willie-Jay upon his release from the Penitentiary, and that it is only after missing Willie-Jay by five hours that Perry consents to partake in Dick's scheme. Symbolically, the planned "score" and the desperate actions that ensue become a kind of substitute for Perry's last chance to reconnect with his "real and only friend," foretelling the extent to which the murders are to act as recompense for his dejected life.

Summary and Analysis of The Last to See Them Alive, Part 1 ...

Summary and Analysis of The Last To See Them Alive, Part 2 (58-74)

Nancy Ewalt, a friend of Nancy Clutter's, arrives at River Valley Farm early on Sunday morning to accompany the family to church. When, after repeated summons, the Clutters fail to answer the door, Nancy drives to town to consult Susan Kidwell, her closest confidante. Unable to arrive at a logical explanation for the Clutters' curious absence, together the girls return to the farm, enter the house, and discover Nancy in her bedroom, dead from a shotgun blast to the head.

The sheriff, police, and town officials descend on the farm and uncover the rest of the family: Bonnie Clutter in her bedroom, also dead from a gunshot to the head; Mr. Clutter and Kenyon, bound and gagged in the basement of the house, the boy shot in the face and Mr. Clutter's throat slit.

The news sends shock waves through the small town, prompting all manner of speculation about the motivation for the crime and the identity of the perpetrator(s). Sue Kidwell and Bobby Rupp are both devastated by the loss of Nancy, and seek solace in each other's company. The extended Clutter family makes the journey to Holcomb, including Beverly and Eveanna, the elder two daughters of Herb and Bonnie.

Meanwhile, having arrived back in Olathe, Perry retires to a hotel room, while Dick returns to his parents' house in time for Sunday dinner and to watch the afternoon basketball game on TV...

Analysis:

The book's first real ellipsis (gap or chronological leap) occurs here, as Capote skips the details of the murders and presents the deaths from the point of view of the Holcomb residents discovering them. This strategy partly reflects the trajectory of Capote's research – the events of the night of November 14th were among the last to be revealed to him, after he had befriended the killers on Death Row – but it also allows the motivation for the murders to remain obscure, and to be revealed gradually as the characters of Dick and Perry are themselves explored in greater depth. At this point, they are still "persons unknown," to the reader as much as to the Kansas authorities, and Capote seems to be implying that no crime can be fully understood without a detailed and sensitive consideration of the persons involved.

The townspeople's reaction to the news of the killings is one of "amazement, shading into dismay; a shallow horror sensation that cold springs of personal fear swiftly deepened" (70). The Clutters' demise has larger significance for this sheltered little part of western Kansas: it amounts to the infiltration of an "other" – a "poor, rootless, misbegotten" other – into their peaceable and prosperous little universe (Clarke, 356). The Clutter killings symbolize a collision of the two sides of

America: the prosperous, self-assured "haves" with the disappointed and destitute "have-nots." The ideology of the American dream is forced to confront those it has left behind.

Summary and Analysis of Persons Unknown, Part 1 (77-123)

A team of detectives from the Kansas Bureau of Investigation (KBI) assembles under the leadership of Alvin Adams Dewey, who takes charge of the case at the special request of the Finney County sheriff. The team also includes Special Agents Harold Nye, Roy Church, and Clarence Duntz. The crime scene provides little in the way of physical evidence – only a few footprints, as well as the materials used to bind the victims – and the team begins to comb the surrounding area for witnesses. The initial investigation yields a few suspects, among them Bobby Rupp, but they are soon dismissed.

The town of Holcomb, following the initial trauma of the grim discovery, begins to confront the longer-term implications of the murders: "This hitherto peaceful congregation of neighbors and old friends had suddenly to endure the unique experience of distrusting each other" (88).

In a Kansas City diner, Perry and Dick read a newspaper report about the crime. Dick is confident that the murder cannot be traced to them, but Perry makes reference to a possible connection – someone by the name of "Floyd" – which flusters Dick.

Perry recalls a recurring dream, in which he is rescued from danger by yellow parrot, who "wings him away to paradise." In the course of his retelling, the narration offers hints of a troubled childhood. Dick ridicules the dream and Perry, whom he recalls from their early days in prison to be overly fretful, sensitive and romantic, "such a kid." Perry, on the other hand, regards Dick's cavalier machismo with a mixture of awe and disdain. In prison, Perry recalls, "he'd wanted Dick's friendship, wanted Dick to 'respect' him, think him 'hard,' as much the 'masculine type' as he had considered Dick to be" (111). For this reason, Perry invented a story about murdering a black roommate with a bicycle chain, after which, sure enough, Dick began to regard him as a possible accomplice, and perhaps even someone to be "afraid of" (109).

The Clutter funeral is well-attended, and Beverly Clutter, the second eldest of the two surviving Clutter children, is married in Holcomb several days later. The investigation begins to take its toll on the family of Alvin Dewey, who develops an obsessive interest in tracking down the perpetrators. In the absence of any real breaks in the case, rumors continue to circulate in the small town, and several prominent families announce their decision to pack up and move out of state.

Perry and Dick begin dropping bogus checks in Kansas City, a spree which affords them enough cash to drive to Mexico. Once there, they briefly team up with a rich German man named Otto and his Acapulcan compatriot, "The Cowboy."

On a December afternoon, Paul Helm, the groundsman at River Valley Farm, discovers an intruder inside the Clutter home. The sheriff apprehends the man, who is identified as Jonathan Daniel Adrian, and who has in his possession a 12-gauge shotgun and a hunting knife. He becomes the principal suspect in the case.

Analysis:

For the first time in the book, Capote foregrounds the relationship between Dick and Perry, and offers clues about Perry's upbringing. The two quibble over the question of whether the crime can be traced to them; in the course of the argument, Perry is hyper-aware of the circumstances and the possibility of rebuke, whereas Dick is self-assured, almost to the point of recklessness. This marks a fundamental point of difference between the two men: Perry, always sizing up the opposition and measuring himself against a persecuting world, and Dick, carefree, barely cognizant of the potential consequences of his actions.

Perry's dream of the yellow parrot – which offers him salvation from the abusive nuns of his childhood, and later from other "tormenting" figures in his life – gives us reason to believe that all of his dreams (of treasure-hunting, of becoming a famous musician) are a kind of coping mechanism, a way of compensating for misfortunes he has suffered. There is a point at which Perry's self-protecting mechanisms become a kind of self-pitying self-aggrandizement, such as when he leaves the poem for Cookie explaining why he must hurt them both by leaving her: "There's a race of men that don't fit in, / A race that can't sit still; / So they break the hearts of kith and kin, / And they roam the world at will…" (98). A tension begins to emerge between Perry's perception of himself as exceptional (even "artistic"), misunderstood, unsuited for conventional living, and the fact that others have, throughout his life, looked down on him, viewed him as inferior or inadequate.

Wanting Dick to think of him as "hard," or "masculine," he has invented a story about murdering a stranger, which, sure enough, impresses Dick. Nevertheless, Dick uses Perry as a foil for his own self-image, belittling him for his superstitions and sensitive outlook, his "childish" fantasies of adventure, and his friendship with the eccentric Willie-Jay. Next to Perry, Dick considers himself to be "a normal." Moreover, Dick has been pretending to go along with Perry's treasure-hunting schemes, not actually believing a word of them or intending to follow through, creating a potentially volatile scenario in which Perry will feel slighted or betrayed when he realizes Dick's true feelings.

The encounter with Otto and the Cowboy has fairly explicit homoerotic overtones. The narrative relates that: "Dick had 'picked him up.' But the gentleman, a vacationing Hamburg lawyer, 'already had a friend'—a young native Acapulcan who called himself the Cowboy" (118). Otto sketches a series of portraits – an act that has implications of sexual voyeurism – including several "nude studies" of Dick. While it is never made overtly clear whether Dick and Perry's relationship is romantic – Capote argued emphatically that it was not – the reader is meant to deduce some sort of erotic tension fueling their interactions.

The episode with Otto also foregrounds the theme of self-image in relation to homoerotic attraction. Freud argued that "a man who seeks other men may be yearning, on some deeper level, to embrace his own self-reflection" (Smith, 232). If Perry and Dick are indeed drawn to one another in this way, it may be the case that, on some level, each wishes narcissistically to see himself in the other person (the book has demonstrated how each admires and envies qualities of the other). Such a vision would be, in a way, self-validating. The same may be said of the relationship between Perry and Truman Capote, although of course this is not featured in the book: that each man saw, in the other, a distorted self-image, a picture of what he might have been.

That the town of Holcomb has experienced a loss of innocence is a point that Capote continues to explore in this section. Disillusioned by the crime, the residents are fraught with feelings of fear and mistrust, and many set off to settle elsewhere, hoping to regain their sense of security and well-being.

In Garden City, Agent Dewey continues to obsess over the materials of the crime, and we are given the first glimpse into the manner in which the killings transpired: the mattress-box underneath Mr. Clutter, the pillow under Kenyon's head, and the fact that Nancy all indicate that the killers felt some sort of empathy for – or personal responsibility toward – their victims.

Summary and Analysis of Persons Unknown, Part 1 (77-123)

Summary and Analysis of Persons Unknown, Part 2 (123-155)

In a Mexico City hotel room, Perry browses through his personal artifacts and papers. He comes across a letter written by his father on his behalf while at the Kansas State Penitentiary, detailing the events of Perry's early life. As one of four children born to the Western rodeo duo of Tex John Smith and Florence Buckskin, Perry lived an impoverished and itinerant childhood until his parents' separation when Perry was six years old. After living for a short while with his alcoholic mother, Perry was sent to a Catholic orphanage, where nuns routinely abused him for wetting the bed. After he contracted pneumonia from this and other forms of neglect, his father took him away to live in Alaska, where he learned to hunt and track, and to search for gold in nearby streams.

As a young man, Perry enlisted in the Merchant Marine and, subsequently, the Army. After several tours of duty, followed by a motorcycle accident that left him badly injured and immobile for six months, he rejoined his father in Alaska. Together they built a hunting lodge which, after all their labor, failed to attract clientele, and after a row with Tex John, Perry departed Alaska again, this time for good. He was subsequently arrested for robbery, which is how he came to be in the Kansas State Penitentiary.

Also among his personal papers is a letter from his sister, Barbara. Barbara is Perry's only surviving sibling; his brother Jimmy and sister Fern have both committed suicide by the time the narrative opens. Barbara lives a comfortable life with her husband and three children in San Francisco, and scolds Perry for his irresponsible lifestyle and disrespect towards their father. Accompanying her letter is a commentary by Willie-Jay ("Impressions I Garnered from the Letter") in which he proposes that Barbara is limited not only by her conventionalism, but by her own frustrations and insecurity related to their family history, and is therefore incapable of empathizing with Perry's situation.

Agent Dewey pays a visit to the Clutter house, as he continues to grapple with the unyielding tangle of events surrounding the case. Jonathan Adrian, we are told, has been cleared of the charge, and Dewey is showing signs of the stress of the unsolved murders.

Dick, dissatisfied with the job opportunities available in Mexico, decides to return to the United States, and the pair make their way slowly north once again.

Analysis:

By the time that Perry and Dick reach the hotel room, Dick has revealed his opinion of Perry's treasure-hunting schemes; and although this declaration "hurt and shocked" Perry it also, surprisingly, "charmed him, almost revived his former faith in the tough, the 'totally masculine,' the pragmatic, the decisive Dick he'd once allowed to boss him" (124). It appears that tension and rivalry, rather than harmony and accord, are ultimately what sustain their relationship, a point that will become significant later when the details of the murders are recounted.

The disappointments and vicissitudes of Perry's early life are here revealed in full, and they have been formative to his current disposition. In particular, the mistreatment and humiliation at the hands of the "Black Widows" at the Catholic orphanage seem to have made a lasting impression on him, contributing to his sensitive outlook (which sometimes borders on paranoia) and his vulnerable self-image. We also learn that Perry's father was emotionally – and literally – absent for large segments of his childhood, and Perry spent his adolescence isolated from his siblings and peers and without a traditional education (another premise for his later inferiority complex).

Perry's sister, like Dick, uses him as a foil to convince herself that her own lifestyle is "normal," and that she has escaped the misfortunes and mental dissolutions of her parents and siblings. Willie-Jay senses that the implicit agenda of her letter is to validate herself, and overcome her own insecurities about their family history by debasing Perry's "unconventional" lifestyle and valorizing their parents. Nevertheless, Willie-Jay's analysis of the letter has the effect of further alienating Perry: Perry internalizes the self-image Willie-Jay projects onto him, that he is beyond the understanding of most ordinary people, and as a result becomes more "antisocial" and isolated than ever.

Perry would like to be a nihilist, to completely discount the value of human life and the importance of those around him. In his journal he has inscribed the quote, "Why worry? What was there to 'sweat about'? Man was nothing, a mist, a shadow absorbed by shadows" (147). But something holds him back from complete abandon: "But, damn it, you do worry, scheme, fret over your fingernails and the warnings of hotel managements"(147). Try as he might, he finds himself unable to let go of the concerns that most rankle him, which often take the form of the reprimands of others.

Following the initial frenzy caused by the crime, the residents of Garden City and Holcomb sink into its gloomy aftermath. Mrs. Dewey recounts a dream in which Bonnie Clutter informs her that there is "nothing worse" than to be murdered, indicating the psychological toll of the experience, even on those not directly involved. Alvin Dewey continues to dwell on the Clutter home, finding it a comforting symbol of quieter time. On some level, it seems, he hopes to find, within the material artifacts of the home, a resolution to the collective trauma that the residents of Garden City have suffered.

Summary and Analysis of Answer, Part 1 (159-215)

The reader is introduced to Floyd Wells for the first time. Wells, a former employee at River Valley Farm, was Dick's first cellmate at the Kansas State Penitentiary, and the first to inform Dick what a "score" might be had by robbing the Clutter household. Upon hearing the news of the murders, he realizes that Dick must be the perpetrator, and presents his account to the authorities at the prison.

The KBI investigative unit is elated to receive this lead, and Agent Nye pays a visit to the parents of Dick Hickcock, who offer some clues about Dick's early life. Though a decent student and talented athlete, as a young man Dick could not afford to attend college. Instead, at the age of nineteen he married a sixteen-year-old girl named Carol, and the pair had three children. They spent several years living above their means and accruing debt, and Dick began to gamble and write bad checks before finally divorcing Carol for another woman. Eventually, Dick was sent to prison for theft, where he met Perry and others. However, for the few months prior to the fateful night of November 14th, Dick had been living peacefully in his parents' home, earning an honest living at the Bob Sands Auto Shop. On that night, he convinced his parents that he would be accompanying Perry to meet Perry's sister in Fort Scott, where she was holding a sum of fifteen hundred dollars for Perry.

Dick and Perry, hitchhiking in Nebraska, hatch a plan to murder and rob the motorists who offer rides to them, but are repeatedly thwarted. Crossing the border into Iowa, they take refuge from a rainstorm in an empty barn, where they find and steal a 1956 Chevrolet. From here they make their way to Kansas City, where Dick goes on another shopping spree with bad checks. Perry is uneasy with the prospect of being so close to the Kansas authorities, and wary of Dick's recklessness, but he complies grudgingly.

The KBI detectives continue to seek out the relatives and acquaintances of Perry and Dick. Agent Nye visits the boardinghouse in Las Vegas where Perry is reported to have stayed, and discovers a cardboard box filled with his possessions. He then seeks out Barbara, Perry's sister, in her San Francisco home, where she admits to being "afraid" of her brother. As children, she relates, they were inseparable, but she became fearful of his "wild" tendencies as he grew into adulthood. Perry, for his part, resents the education that Barbara and their two other siblings received while he was confined to trapping furs with his father in Alaska.

The Kansas City police, meanwhile, have identified the stolen Chevrolet, which has been traced to the fugitives. Dick and Perry have made their way to Miami Beach with the earnings from Dick's spree, where they spend Christmas. Dick flirts with a young girl on the beach, which Perry observes with disgust: Perry has "no respect for people who can't control themselves sexually."

The murders continue to haunt the town of Holcomb. Bobby Rupp and Susan Kidwell mourn the loss of their friend during the holiday season, and Bobby reminisces about happy Christmas days spent at the Clutter house. Dick and Perry continue to roam the countryside, one day meeting up with an old man and his grandson, who teach them to collect bottles on the roadside to exchange for refund deposits.

On the evening of December 30th, Alvin Dewey receives a phone call, informing him that Perry Smith and Dick Hickock have been arrested in Las Vegas. The Dewey family is at once jubilant to hear of this victory, and apprehensive for what is to come.

Analysis:

After learning so much about Perry's early life, we are now offered Dick's story. His criminal (or "antisocial") tendencies are in some ways harder to explain than Perry's, or at least, they don't have roots in childhood neglect. Dick has a solid home life, and genuine affection for parents and brother. Economic duress seems to have played a bigger role in determining Dick's chosen path, but the decisive event seems to have been a head injury he received in a car accident, after which, according to his father, he "wasn't the same boy."

Dick's mother makes a comment about Perry that again foregrounds the topic of homosexuality: "I wouldn't have him in the house. One look and I saw what he was. With his perfume. And his oily hair. It was clear as day where Dick had met him" (169). Although this is not always the determining element of Perry and Dick's relationship, it continues to surface and inflect the reader's perception of events. And in this case, it renders Perry a social outcast; whether or not we choose to believe that the men are romantically involved, homosexuality functions as a symbol of Perry and Dick's larger alienation from conventional society.

Agent Nye gains poignant insight into the life of Perry Smith vis-à-vis a box of his possessions: "True, it was valueless stuff even to a clue-hungry detective. Still, Nye was glad to have seen it; each item—the palliatives for sore gums, the greasy Honolulu pillow—gave him a clearer impression of the owner and his lonely, mean life" (178). Like the artifacts in the Clutter household, these material traces are a weak approximation of the human lives they accompany; but, like the Clutters' possessions, they are the best that can be done when the truth is so remote or so difficult to understand.

Barbara, Perry's sister, has made a life for herself that resembles the Clutters', and she dreads the encroachment of the other world that Perry represents, a world of savagery, resentment, poverty, and self-destruction. She and Perry are divided on the question of their father: Barbara respects and admires Tex John, but Perry harbors deep resentment, blaming him for stunting his intellectual development: "I happen to have a brilliant mind. In case you didn't know. . . . But no education, because he didn't want me to learn anything, only how to tote and carry for him. Dumb. Ignorant. That's the way he wanted me to be" (185). The fact that Perry missed this chance in life has left him bitter, frustrated, and transient; the fact that Barbara did not has enabled her to settle into comfortable and respectable living. The association between Barbara and the Clutters is established in a thoughtful moment of Perry's: "One fine day he'd pay her back, have a little fun—talk to her, advertise his abilities, spell out in detail the things he was capable of doing to people like her, respectable people, safe and smug people, exactly like Bobo" (194).

In Al Dewey's dream, the killers are elevated to an epic, inhuman, invincible stature – the mythology of the unsolved crime. As fugitives, they are the essence of evil, wreaking havoc on the innocent; as prisoners (as they will shortly become), they will be revealed in all their frailty and broken humanity; Capote sets up a deliberate contrast by presenting them as larger-than-life in the dream, only to undermine this perception in the scenes to follow.

In the Miami Beach episode, Dick's insecurities are bared. First, he observes a wealthy man of his age, and wonders, "Why should that sonofabitch have everything, while he had nothing?" (201). Later, on the beach, he succumbs to a tendency of which he is most "sincerely ashamed," his sexual interest in young girls, by attempting to lure a twelve-year-old. Perry, ever watchful, is disgusted by this behavior.

As the stress of the journey wears on them, the fugitives' personalities begin to polarize. Perry becomes more apprehensive, and more self-admonishing, whereas Dick starts taking bigger risks. The friction between the two of them begins to escalate, a development which is probably based at least partly on the men's actual experiences while traveling together. But it also functions as a narrative tactic: Capote builds the drama leading up to the climactic revelation of the events of November 14th, during which, as we will learn, the rivalry between the men literally exploded and resulted in the deaths of the four Clutters.

This, in turn, begs a larger question that has occupied Capote's critics and readers alike: to what extent is In Cold Blood a simple recounting of fact, and to what extent is it shaped by Capote's own interpretation of the events and his literary designs?

Summary and Analysis of Answer, Part 2 (215-248)

Interrogation of the two suspects begins. The detectives initially withhold any mention the Clutter case, and allow Dick and Perry to assume they are being held for parole violation. The pair have agreed upon an alibi for the night of November 14th, which they confidently present to the questioning parties. After several hours, the detectives come forth with the real reason for the questioning: that Perry and Dick are wanted for quadruple homicide, an accusation which catches both men off guard (Dick more so than Perry). They are relegated to jail cells at opposite ends of the building.

In subsequent rounds of interrogation, the detectives present the evidence against the two men: Floyd Wells' testimony, along with the two sets of footprints found at the crime scene, which perfectly match two pairs of boots in the duo's possession. In a panic, Dick accuses Perry of the murders: "It was Perry. I couldn't stop him. He killed them all."

The residents of Holcomb receive the news of the arrest with ambivalence. Feelings of relief are mitigated by doubts as to whether Dick and Perry are solely to blame for the murders: "Some day they'll get to the bottom, and when they do they'll find the one behind it. The one wanted Clutter out of the way. The brains" (231).

On the way from Las Vegas to Garden City, Dewey mentions to Perry the story of the bicycle-chain killing, whereby Perry realizes that Dick has confessed all: "I thought it was a stunt. I didn't believe you. That Dick let fly. . . .I always knew if we ever got caught, if Dick ever really let fly, dropped his guts all over the goddam floor—I knew he'd tell about the nigger" (232). Perry makes a lengthy confession of his own, but claims that Dick was responsible for two of the four killings.

According to Perry, the duo had arrived at River Valley convinced – on the basis of Floyd Wells' testimony – that Herb Clutter kept a safe loaded with ten thousand dollars inside the house. Upon entering the house and finding no such safe, they roused Mr. Clutter from his ground-level bedroom, demanding to know where the cash was kept. Mr. Clutter denied the existence of the safe or of any large sum on the premises, offering a scant thirty dollars to the robbers.

Making their way upstairs, Perry continues, the men demanded whatever money the other members of the family had. After binding and taping the family members in the rooms where they were eventually found, Dick continued to search for a safe, while Perry chatted in a friendly manner with the hostages. At one point, Dick proposed to rape Nancy Clutter, to which Perry responded, "Uh-huh. But you'll have to kill me first."

At this point Perry describes the exchange that led to the eventual killing spree:

"He was holding the knife. I asked him for it, and I said, 'All right, Dick. Here goes.' But I didn't mean it. I meant to call his bluff, make him argue me out of it, make him admit he was a phony and a coward. See, if was something between me and Dick. I knelt down beside Mr. Clutter, and the pain of kneeling . . . the shame. Disgust. . . . But I didn't realize what I'd done till I heard the sound. Like somebody drowning. Screaming under the water" (244).

The three other murders, Perry relates, transpired in quick succession in a blind frenzy on the part of the killers. All told, the pair made off with "between forty and fifty dollars."

The motorcade transporting Dick and Perry arrives in Garden City. A large crowd has been waiting throughout the day to see them into the courthouse, and the town officials expect the congregation to be rowdy and abusive to the men. However, "when the crowd caught sight of the murderers, with their escort of blue-coated highway patrol-men, it fell silent, as though amazed to find them humanly shaped" (248).

Analysis:

Perry's confession is in some sense the climactic sequence of In Cold Blood, in spite of the fact that it refers to events that have already taken place. All the narrative threads of the book up to this point have anticipated this release of information: it satisfies the KBI investigators' search for an explanation of what happened on the night of the killings, and in a subtler way, it completes the picture of Dick and Perry that the narrative has so carefully traced throughout the book.

Perhaps the most important fact that emerges is that the killings were not determined by either man acting of his own resolve, but by a dynamic exchange between Dick and Perry's competing personalities. Perry puts a stop to Dick's sexual conquest of Nancy, which adds to the frustration of the moment and heightens the stakes of finding the safe. Perry almost leaves the scene at several points, but Dick urges him to remain, even after it becomes clear that there is no safe in the house. Yet, in spite of Dick's persuasion, we learn that Perry is the one who finally initiates the murders. Perry describes the final moments leading up to the killings as a kind of competitive show-down between himself and Dick: "I meant to call his bluff, make him argue me out of it, make him admit he was a phony and a coward" (244). We can be fairly certain that the decision to kill the Clutters would not have been made if the two men had not spent the evening at odds with each other, and if the situation had not produced more feelings of frustration and impotence than it alleviated.

If a decision to kill was made, it was clearly Perry who made it; yet his account gives us reason to believe that the action was somehow automatic or unconscious, carried out while Perry was deep in a reverie of shame and self-loathing. This point is formally recognized and explored in greater depth in Perry's psychiatric evaluation for the trial; but what is most important to note is that the robbery, which was supposed to restore the men's dignity and self-determination, in fact makes Perry feel more helpless and contemptible than ever. Momentarily, he assigns the blame for his self-loathing to Herb Clutter, and all four Clutters pay the ultimate price for his pain.

In Cold Blood is often described as highly cinematic or visually appealing, nowhere more pronouncedly than in this confession sequence, in which the narrative is operating on two levels at ones (the reader is, on the one hand, in the car with Agents Dewey and Duntz, and on the other, in the Clutter house on the fateful night). Capote's attention to detail smoothes over the gaps that might have been present in a more traditional journalistic account, and does a lot of legwork to convince the reader of the truth of the facts being recounted. Yet, for much of this sequence, we are inside the head of Perry Smith, and our own experience of the events of that night is filtered through his subjective perceptions, just as the text of In Cold Blood is filtered through the perceptions of the Truman Capote. In spite of the book's realism, it is important to remember the place of the author, and to consider that even the most straightforward sequence of facts may be rearranged to lend multiple shades of meaning.

Summary and Analysis of The Corner, Part 1 (248-307)

Dick and Perry are confined to separate quarters of the Finney County jailhouse. Dick occupies a cell in the men's wing, while Perry resides adjacent to the Sheriff's residence, in the cell typically reserved for female convicts. Several months pass, during which the state-appointed defense attorneys prepare their cases. Dick and Perry make official statements, and Perry revises his confession to read that he (Perry) pulled the trigger on all four victims (this, he confides, is done not out of concern for Dick but out of respect for Dick's beleaguered parents). Dick and Perry's advocates arrange for a psychiatric evaluation of the two men, which is performed by a young doctor named W. Mitchell Jones. One week before the trial is set to begin in Garden City, an auction is held at River Valley Farm, and all of the Clutters' possessions are sold.

The trial begins, and the testimonies are heard from Sue Kidwell, Nancy Ewalt, and various other residents and officials of Holcomb; Floyd Wells; the four K.B.I. agents, including Alvin Dewey; Mr. Hickock; and finally, Dr. Jones.

In his psychiatric evaluations of the two men, Dr. Jones has uncovered a number of explanatory details. Dick, he concludes, shows signs of "emotional abnormality," which may be a sign of brain damage incurred in a car accident as a young man. Feelings of social and sexual inadequacy are at the root of many of Dick's more reckless criminal actions; in short, Dick shows "fairly typical characteristics of what would psychiatrically be called a severe character disorder" (295).

Even more pronouncedly, Perry "shows definite signs of severe mental illness." Neglected as a child, he has developed a "'paranoid' orientation toward the world," and "in evaluating the intentions and feelings of others, his ability to separate the real intention from his own mental projections is very poor." Perhaps most significant is his "poorly controlled rage—easily triggered by any feeling of being tricked, slighted or labeled inferior to others." His personality traits, in other words, most closely resemble that of a paranoid schizophrenic.

Having made these diagnoses, however, Dr. Jones is unable to present them in full at the trial; the court's criteria for establishing criminal intent does not encompass these more implicit and indirect psychological factors. However, in an article published around the time of the trial, a colleague of Dr. Jones, Dr. Joseph Statten, makes a similar psychological evaluation of four other convicted murderers: namely, that after experiencing "severe emotional deprivation" in childhood, and feelings of inadequacy throughout their lives, these men committed atrocities of violence while in a detached frame of mind. Dr. Statten concludes that the killers unconsciously made their victims into a kind of surrogate object of blame for their previous life traumas.

Perry is visited by Don Cullivan, an old friend from his Army days who, upon hearing the news of Perry's arraignment, volunteers to testify as a "character witness" for Perry. Cullivan, a devout Catholic, dines with Perry and attempts to comfort him with thoughts of God's mercy. Perry admits that he is not bothered by the murders and is hence unable to feel remorse.

In the closing remarks of the trial, the beleaguered defense lawyers appeal to the mercy of the jury, attempting to dissuade them from exacting the highest form of punishment. After a forty-minute deliberation, the jury finds both Dick and Perry guilty on four counts of murder in the first degree, and sentence them both to death.

Analysis:

After the book's extensive exploration of the personalities of Dick and Perry, the professional findings of Dr. Jones come as no surprise, but they carry their own weight nonetheless. Dr. Jones uncovers a clinical basis for many of the their more pronounced traits, including the behaviors that played a direct role in the events of November 14th.

In particular, the murder of Herb Clutter becomes transparent: the patriarch of the Clutter family symbolized, for Perry, all the frustrations and missed opportunities of his own life. As he says later in the book, "I didn't have anything against them, and they never did anything wrong to me--the way other people have all my life. Maybe they're just the ones who had to pay for it." Herb Clutter represents "'a key figure in some past traumatic configuration': his father? the orphanage nuns who had derided and beaten him? the hated army sergeant? the parole officer who had ordered him to 'stay out of Kansas'? One of them, or all of them" (302). As well, Perry's trance-like state ("mental eclipse") while committing the murders is accounted for as a common experience of those with his background and psychological disposition.

This complex and nuanced interpretation of Perry and Dick's psychological makeup invites sympathy rather than condemnation, and this may be part of the reason that the testimony of Dr. Jones is denied during the trial. The prisoners are held to the simplistic M'Naghten rule, which contends that if the defendant knows his actions were wrong by the "usual definitions of right and wrong," then he is responsible for them. This is opposed to the more lenient Durham rule, which claims that defendants cannot be held responsible if the crime is the result of a mental defect (which would, if upheld, exonerate the two prisoners).

The court's inability or unwillingness to sustain Dr. Jones' testimony is, on some level, a symbol that the world is not yet ready to accommodate the complexity and fundamental difference of these men within its narrow definitions of acceptable society. Dick and Perry are social misfits on multiple levels: their mental illness, their implied repressed homosexuality, and their status as ex-convicts place them outside the accepted parameters of conventional (or "normal") living as they existed at this time in American history. They are the very definition of "other," and the comfortable, complacent world that the Clutters represent has turned its back on them, shown no responsibility towards them. In Cold Blood is, on some level, a parable about a society coming of age, failing to cater to its more destitute ranks, and coming face-to-face with the consequences of this failure.

In a moment of sympathy for Perry, Agent Dewey reflects that "the crime was a psychological accident, virtually an impersonal act" (245). Nevertheless, in the same moment he is seized by the realization of the horror experienced by the Clutters at the hands of these men: "They had experienced prolonged terror, they had suffered." In spite of its understanding of the killers and their motivation, the book remains ambivalent on the subject of the crime itself, as it sees the killers through their very last days.

Summary and Analysis of The Corner, Part 2 (307-343)

Dick and Perry are transferred to Death Row at the Kansas State Penitentiary, a small "coffin-shaped" building at one end of the prison compound. Among their fellow inmates is Lowell Lee Andrews, a former honors student at the University of Kansas who has been found guilty of the brutal and calculated murders of his parents and older sister. Much like Dick and Perry's case, the Andrews case "became the basis for a legal and medical crusade," in which lawyers attempted, unsuccessfully, to use Andrews's psychological imbalance as a defense against imprisonment and the death penalty.

Dick and Perry's relationship has become one of "mutual toleration," and despite living in adjacent cells, they hardly communicate with one another, because Perry doesn't like being overheard by the other inmates and guards. Perry especially dislikes Andrews, who is better educated than him and often corrects his grammar.

By the beginning of June, Perry has stopped eating, and spends the summer in the prison hospital, connected to a feeding tube yet still refusing sustenance, determined to take his own life before it can be taken from him. One afternoon, however, he receives a card from his father, addressed to the warden, inquiring about his son; the card inspires a frenzy of "love and hate," and Perry resolves to end his fast and return to the world of the living.

Two years pass, along with several postponements of the execution date. Two teenagers, Ronnie York and James Latham, who have been convicted of a serial murder rampage across the United States, join the row.

Dick writes a number of appeals arguing that he and Perry have not had a fair trial, one of which catches the eye of Everett Steerman, the Chairman of the Legal Aid Committee at the Kansas Bar Association. As a result, the Bar Association conducts a series of hearings, which are essentially intended to protect the reputation of the Kansas Courts rather than to rehash the murder case. The investigating attorney, Russell Shultz, finds little evidence supporting Dick's claims of an unfair trial, and the Judge issues a new date of execution, October 25, 1962. This date, in the end, passes by harmlessly, but Andrews is hanged a month later.

In a long soliloquy in the final pages of the book, Dick describes the death of Andrews, and how Perry "wasn't sorry to see the last of Andy." He describes Perry as lonely and bitter, never receiving visitors except "the journalist" (Capote), and jealous of any correspondence that Dick receives.

Three more years pass, and Shultz's replacements, Joseph P. Jenkins and Robert Bingham, file several more appeals to postpone the execution date. The case reaches the United States Supreme Court three times, but is denied a hearing in each instance. Finally, the Kansas Supreme Court sets the date for April 14th, 1965.

The focus shifts to Agent Dewey, from whose perspective the final few scenes of the book are presented. He attends the execution, to watch first Dick, then Perry (like a "creature walking wounded") finally meet their demise. Poignantly, Perry's final words are, "It would be meaningless to apologize for what I did. Even inappropriate. But I do. I apologize."

The narrative rewinds to the previous May, where it finds Dewey weeding his father's grave in the Garden City cemetery. He reflects on the events of the previous four years: the passing of Judge Tate and other members of the community, and the recent marriage of Bobby Rupp. Wandering over to the Clutters' grave, he finds Susan Kidwell, who is a junior at the University of Kansas, and is back for a visit to Holcomb. They converse about the passage of time and the more recent events of their lives, and she finally departs, leaving Dewey to the "whisper of wind voices in the wind-bent wheat" (343).

Analysis:

The introduction of Lowell Lee Andrews throws the characters of Dick and Perry into relief once more. On the one hand, Andrews' criminality is described in much simpler terms than the other two: unlike Perry and Dick – whose criminal tendencies have been the result of a complex interplay of environmental factors, and for whom murder comes as a "psychological accident" – Andrews' murderous impulses are described as basic to his nature. He is an otherwise ordinary boy whose one outstanding feature is that "it seemed to him just as right to kill his mother as to kill an animal or a fly" (316).

On the other hand, Lowell Lee has much in common with Dick and Perry: both the Andrews and the Clutter cases are ambiguous from a legal and moral standpoint, for Andrews, like Dick and Perry, suffers from a diagnosable mental condition that played a very direct role in his decision to carry out the murders. And, as with Dick and Perry, the courts have been unsympathetic to these complicating factors; Andrews is another person whom the system has "left behind," who has proven, in some sense, too complex or cumbersome to be accommodated.

As the prisoners on the row are forced to confront the reality of their own impending deaths, each conducts himself in a characteristic fashion. Perry, who hates to think of himself at the mercy of the authorities, attempts to take matters into his own hands by starving himself. Dick, ever the pragmatist, accepts the sentence calmly, even good-naturedly, but concocts a number of schemes to free himself, including the appeals to the Kansas Bar Association. Andrews is by far the most complacent among them, declaring that "sooner or later we'll all get out of here. Either walk out—or be carried out in a coffin. Myself, I don't care whether I walk or get carried" (318).

While the majority of the text has been dedicated to the eight weeks following the murders – the investigation, pursuit, and trial of the killers – a scant few pages remain to describe the comparatively vast expanse of time that the prisoners are on death row; indeed, these five years are something of an afterthought. In part, the clipped pace of this last section is a testament to the tedium of the cell block (the details of the prisoners' day-to-day existence are hardly worth the space they would occupy on the page), but it is also an implicit testimonial to the value that society places on these men after their condemnation. Locked away, they are soon forgotten, such that even the narrative seems ready to be rid of them. (Capote, too, was anxious for the execution day to arrive, having sacrificed a great deal – including his mental health – in order to see the story through to completion.)

Nevertheless, Capote's undeniable affection for the prisoners begins to show in the final pages. So careful to keep himself out of the narrative up to this point, he allows himself to appear twice in a conversation with Dick (as "the journalist"), in one of the last scenes of the book. Historically speaking, at this point in his research, he was more enmeshed with Perry and Dick than ever, and at last he seems tacitly to acknowledge his own agency in shaping the events of the story (for it is true that he played a significant role in the prisoners' lives during these final few years).

The final episode, with Alvin Dewey in the graveyard, is one of the only fictional scenes in the book. Capote wanted to end In Cold Blood on a hopeful note, and so he invented the exchange between Dewey and Sue Kidwell (a move that earned him a great deal of criticism, from reviewers who otherwise applauded the book). Nevertheless, Capote wanted to use this scene to make a final point: that life persists, and time marches forward, even in the aftermath of such great upheaval and tragedy. Both Dewey and Sue Kidwell are in the process of looking back, but they are also oriented toward the future. Even the landscape, with which Capote began the narrative and with which he now concludes it, offers a poignant reminder that the seasons – like human life itself – come and go with the passing years.

Suggested Essay Questions

1. **Capote, when asked whether he was conscious of "film techniques" in *In Cold Blood*, responded "not at all." Why might some consider the book to be cinematic? In what ways is *In Cold Blood* more like a movie than a novel, and what does this contribute to our overall understanding of the book's themes?**

The book is arranged as a series of small scenes or vignettes, punctuated by breaks in the narrative resembling "cuts," which weave together several plotlines. Dialogue is reproduced verbatim, minimizing Capote's authorial intervention and drawing the reader closer to the action. On top of this, his attention to the physical details of his characters and the spaces they occupy makes the book very visually appealing, in a way that mimics the photographic gaze. *In Cold Blood* is, in many ways, the story of a community coming of age in modernity, and of the catastrophe that occurs when two worlds collide. It is appropriate, then, that Capote would craft his novel like a film, the quintessentially modern medium. Films, by virtue of their total sensory grasp over their audiences, also invite the identification of their viewers more readily than any other medium; so by utilizing film techniques, Capote manipulates the structures of identification necessary to secure their sympathy for the killers.

2. **What is the role of family in *In Cold Blood*? Choose two or three characters and compare and contrast how family relationships have shaped or defined them. Does the integrity of a family symbolize something larger in the context of the book?**

For the most part, within the context of Capote's book, the strength of a family seems to stem from and depend on self-determination, social status, and financial security. The Clutters are the strongest family group, and they also hold the highest position on the socioeconomic ladder. Perry, on the other hand, comes from a broken home, which helps to explain his desperate situation in the world. And Dick associates financial security with family, pledging that he will return to his first wife and their children after he has placed himself on solid financial footing. This may be because the two structures determine each other: the integrity of family dictates the strength of the individual to withstand outside pressures, while at the same time one's ability to conquer the pressures of the world determines how unified one's family will be.

3. **Despite the fact that Capote spent years with the killers and the residents of Finney County, and developed close personal ties to many of them, he is almost entirely absent from the narrative. Or is he? Are there places where his point of view creeps into the book? What literary devices does he develop to convince the reader that he is present or absent from the story?**

Capote allows himself to appear in the final section of the book, while describing events in which he played a very direct role. Otherwise, the book aspires to present a perfectly objective and disinterested account of the events of the case; Capote's attention to detail and his ability to reproduce dialogue verbatim gives the book a hyper-real quality, glossing his authorial sleight of hand and allowing the reader to feel as though he or she is experiencing the events firsthand, unfiltered by the author's point of view. Nevertheless, Capote himself admitted that in spite of the book's realistic pretensions, it is a highly subjectivized, opinionated account; authors of so-called non-fiction narratives simply control the meaning of the story "by the selection of what you choose to tell."

4. **What is the role of religion in the book? Are Perry and Dick entirely without religious beliefs? If so, can it be said that they are operating by an alternative moral code? How would you describe this?**

Both Perry and Dick have little tolerance for traditional religion: Dick has never been compelled by a concept of God, and despite being momentarily swayed by the pious Willie-Jay, Perry ultimately cannot forgive the hypocrisy of the nuns who brutalized him as a child. The conceit is that organized religion is a self-serving apparatus of the rich and powerful (or the merely powerful, in the case of the nuns), and that its version of morality excludes the likes of Perry and Dick. The attempted robbery momentarily passes for a kind of higher poetic justice for the tribulations of the robbers' own lives, but it is quickly transformed into an act that is morally reprehensible by any standard. Still, the book tempts us to sympathize with the killers, and to suspend the normal criteria by which we judge the morality of an act.

5. **Discuss the role of dreams or fantasies in the book. What causes a person to have dreams or fantasies, and how do they influence a person's course of action? How do these dreams compare with reality?**

For this question, one may choose to focus on Perry's yellow parrot dream (or his fantasies about treasure hunting, or becoming a famous musician); Dick's hope of becoming financially solvent and returning as the patriarch of his family; and/or the more implicit fantasy of the "American dream" that the Clutter lifestyle embodies. Perry's dreams are the furthest removed from reality and thus the most unrealizable (it may be useful to explore why this is so), and it is ultimately he who is driven to the most extreme criminal actions. Dick's dreams, though more pragmatic, also go largely unfulfilled, and this certainly relates to his criminality. The Clutters, by contrast, have attained everything to which they have aspired, and this underpins their upstanding lifestyle. For this essay, one might explore the relationship between personal wish-fulfillment and the ability to live a normal life within the boundaries of acceptable society, and/or the extent to which dreams determine one's life circumstances and vice versa.

6. **Discuss the role of gender in the relationship between Dick and Perry. How does each man conform to, or deviate from, traditional gender norms? How does each man use the other to define his own gender identity? Does gender – and in particular, masculinity – symbolize something larger in the context of the book?**

Each man uses the other as a foil for his own self-conception: Dick feminizes Perry in order to maintain his own masculine identity, while, unaware of this, Perry looks to Dick for affirmation that he, too, is "hard," or "the masculine type." Perry's more effeminate qualities, as reflected in Dick's perception of him – his superstitions, his sensitive and thoughtful disposition – are balanced by the fact that he summons the courage and rage to carried out all four murders. On the other hand, Dick's masculine bravado is revealed to be a way of compensating for deeper insecurities and feelings of sexual and social inadequacy, which are symbolically manifested in his inability to carry out the murders. For Dick and Perry, masculinity is connected to independence, self-determination, and security, while femininity connotes dependency, ineptitude, and instability.

7. **Just before he is hanged, Perry finally apologizes for the crime; however, critical accounts suggest that Capote embellished this part of the novel for dramatic effect, and that the real Perry said nothing of the sort. What do you make of this apology? Discuss why Capote might have invented this segment. Is it faithful to the representation of Perry that the book has crafted up to this point? Does you feel it helps to clarify his character, or makes him more ambiguous? Does knowing that Capote embellished Perry's character in this way cast doubt on the story as a whole?**

This essay may choose to deal with the larger problem of Capote's reportage in *In Cold Blood*. Certainly the apology is inconsistent with the characterization of Perry that we see up to this point (recall the episode with Don Cullivan, in which Perry claims to have no remorse for the killings). The apology, rather, seems to be a last-ditch effort to make Perry into a sympathetic character, which partly reflects the author's personal feelings about him. This essay may focus on other ways in which the reader has been made to feel sympathy for the killers, and reflect on whether this sympathetic portrayal constitutes an objective "truth," or whether it is a manipulation of fact to serve Capote's authorial (and personal) agenda. Do you think the nonfiction novel captures more of the truth than a regular journalistic piece, or do you feel that it is more one-sided? If Capote's version is not the unadulterated truth, discuss how such truth might be attained.

8. **In undertaking his research in Kansas, Capote's original aim was to document the psychological impact of the killings on the residents of Holcomb, only afterwards shifting his focus to Perry and Dick. Describe this impact as it becomes expressed over the course of the**

book. How does Capote directly and indirectly articulate a change in the community? To what extent are the residents of Holcomb responsible for a change in the general milieu, and to what extent are they affected by the goings on around them?

For this essay, it will be useful to focus on the scenes that don't revolve around the investigation and the main characters (Perry, Dick, and the detectives), for example, the scenes in Hartman's Café, or involving Susan Kidwell and Bobby Rupp. Several of the book's secondary characters – Myrtle Clare, Mrs. Ashida, Susan, and Bobby, among others – personify the diverse reactions of the townspeople as a whole to the murders. By studying these characters, it may be possible to form an overarching thesis about the impact of the crime on the surrounding community. It will also be important to observe the way that townspeople symbiotically feed one another's reactions to the crimes. Finally, one should pay attention to how the murders are not always the direct *cause* of unrest, but rather a catalyst or excuse to express sentiments and fears that have already been brewing in the community.

9. **What is the function of sexuality in the novel? Choose three characters and discuss how sexuality operates with and against their values, their sense of themselves, and their personal aspirations. In particular, how does sexuality interact with the concept of family? Are they at odds with one another?**

Dick and Perry place a high premium on "normal" sexuality in the context of the book, which carries with it the connotation of reproduction, childrearing and family, as well as the accompanying virtues of self-determination and socioeconomic stability. In fact, sexual "normalcy" becomes so overstated that it belies the homoerotic undertones of their relationship, as well as Dick's sexual deviance when it comes to young girls. Sexuality is dangerously poised as, on the one hand, an agent of family and wholesome living, and on the other hand, an avenue of deviance, degeneracy and criminality. As well, Herb Clutter's ambivalence about Nancy's relationship with Bobby is stated to be a matter of religion, but we might read against the grain of the text and argue that it has more to do with the specter of sexuality that Bobby introduces into Nancy's otherwise wholesome life. In a larger sense, raising a family carries with it the dangerous requirement of sexuality, which compromises (or else, exposes a measure of hypocrisy in) the holistic ideology of the Clutters and the virtuous Holcombites.

10. **Does the book make a distinction between what is legal and what is moral? Discuss how the book handles the relationship between law and morality with respect to one of the following: the death penalty; the insanity defense (M'Naghten vs. Durham rule); Perry's reckoning with organized religion.**

Capote skillfully manipulates the reader's sympathies against the simple rule of law and/or the dictates of organized religion, showing how neither of these entities adequately responds to the moral exigencies of the Clutter murders. He challenges the death penalty, attempting to demonstrate the hypocrisy and inhumanity of this ruling (as another kind of murder in itself). He also disputes the simplistic M'Naghten rule, by concluding that Perry was *not* truly in control of his mind at the time of the killings. With regard to organized religion, Perry's early encounter with the nuns at the orphanage demonstrates a certain moral ineptitude on the part of organized religion, which causes Perry (and by association, the reader) to turn away from the church and God in search of alternative moral pursuits, ones related to philosophic reflection and personal self-betterment.

In Cold Blood Onscreen: Capote and the Cinematic Gaze

Rarely is the relationship of the writer to his subject matter so interesting, or so relevant, as in the case of Truman Capote's friendship with Perry Smith and Dick Hickock. While he was writing *In Cold Blood*, Capote visited the prisoners regularly and developed a particularly close connection to Perry Smith, which greatly influenced his approach to the subject of his novel, and had a tremendous impact on him personally and professionally. But it is only in recent years that this relationship has been made explicit in the public consciousness, which is partly owing to the release of two films on the subject, Bennett Miller's *Capote* (2005) and Douglas McGrath's *Infamous* (2006).

Given that *In Cold Blood* is often described as "cinematic" – the book's episodic structure and its quick transitions between multiple plotlines make it read more like a movie than a classical novel – it seems almost inevitable that the story would be adapted for the screen. And indeed it was: shortly after the book's publication in 1966, it was optioned by Irving Lazar, filmed under the direction of Richard Brooks, and finally released in December of 1967. The film faithfully reproduces the novel; however, it was criticized at the time of its release for its languid storytelling and heavy-handed approach to the question of capital punishment, and ultimately, as Gerald Clarke recounts, it has "little of the book's impact." Perhaps most significantly, "it is also less cinematic than the book" (386).

Clarke's last remark is illuminating, for the original film adaptation misses many of the subtler registers of Capote's storytelling that mark it as truly cinematic. What the book has in common with the medium of film – and what the two more recent movies about Capote succeed in capturing – is the nature of film's relationship to its subjects, which is based on the concept of the "gaze."

When film critics speak about the cinematic gaze, they are referring to the omnipresent "look" or point-of-view of the camera, which allows the audience to become voyeurs (or unseen onlookers) to the events onscreen. According to theorists, the gaze enables the audience to have two kinds of experience while watching the film. On the one hand, they make the characters onscreen into objects of sexual or libidinous desire (which is fairly understandable, given that movie stars tend to be sexually appealing). On the other hand, the audience members identify with the characters onscreen, narcissistically projecting their own self-image onto that of another, often idealized person (i.e. a movie star). The audience may alternate between these two sensations while watching a film, or sometimes, more subtly, they may experience these feelings of identification and desire simultaneously.

The gaze, so revealing of cinema as a medium, is also a very useful concept for describing Truman Capote's approach to the characters of Perry Smith and Dick Hickock while writing the book. In many ways Capote is the "camera" in the world of the book: he records the events of the murder case from a seemingly omniscient vantage point, without ever revealing his own involvement. But, as the two films about him make explicit, Capote also becomes drawn into his own apparatus, as a kind of spectator, fascinated by the spectacle before him that was only partly his own creation. *Infamous* depicts the relationship between Capote and Perry as driven by romantic and sexual desire, which they consummate physically in the course of the film. *Capote*, on the other hand, does not portray the men as physically intimate, but suggests that the relationship is based on strong feelings of identification, with each man recognizing an image of himself in the other man. As Philip Seymour Hoffman as Capote says late in the film, "It's as if Perry and I grew up in the same house. And one day, he stood up and went out the back door, while I went out the front." According to Harper Lee, speaking about Capote's real-life relationship with Perry Smith, "Each looked at the other and saw – or thought he saw – the man he might have been."

These film renditions shed considerable light on the nature of Capote's storytelling in the context of the book. In a sense, all narration like Capote's has implications of voyeurism, and of making the book's subjects into objects of one's desire. But alongside this, the author himself becomes implicated as a subject in the book, insofar as his depictions of his subjects are also, at the same time, reflections of himself. This criticism of Capote's style has certainly been current since the book's publication, but the films go one step further by exploring its explicit connection to Capote's "offscreen" romance (physical or not) with Perry Smith.

Author of ClassicNote and Sources

Grace Laubacher, author of ClassicNote. Completed on July 21, 2009, copyright held by GradeSaver.

Updated and revised Damien Chazelle July 31, 2009. Copyright held by GradeSaver.

Plimpton, George, ed. Truman Capote: In Which Friends, Enemies, Acquaintances, and Detractors Recall His Turbulent Career. New York: Doubleday, 1997.

Clarke, Gerald. Capote: A Biography. New York: Simon and Schuster, 1988.

Wolfe, Tom. The New Journalism. New York: Harper and Row, 1973.

Lebeau, Vicky. Psychoanalysis and Cinema: The Play of Shadows. London; New York: Wallflower, 2001.

Wood, Michael. "The New Journalism: Review." The New York Times (Books Section). 22 June, 1973.

Allmendinger, Blake. "The Queer Frontier." In Smith, Patricia Juliana. ed: The Queer Sixties. New York: Routledge, 1999.

Maloney, J.J. "In Cold Blood: A Dishonest Book." Crime Magazine, 1999.

http://www.crimemagazine.com/CrimeBooks/incold.htm

Essay: In Cold Blood: Retaining the Reader's Interest through Suspense and Tension

by Amit Momaya
August 12, 2002

In modern literature, suspense and tension are almost essential in producing works that are both successful and interesting to the reader. These two aspects of literature are especially important in Truman Capote's novel, In Cold Blood, which delineates the story of how a mere robbery attempt concludes in the death of four well-respected and affable family members. Although the reader is cognizant of various outcomes in the story beforehand, Capote effectively retains the reader's interest through suspense and tension. Capote particularly engenders this suspense and tension by shifting between simultaneous events, waiting to disclose the details of the murder, and suggesting fallacies in America's judicial system.

Suspense proves to be an essential aspect to this novel, particularly in the way in which it proves to be a new plot mechanism. For example, one way Capote introduces suspense is through the short segments within each chapter. He constantly switches back and forth between Dick and Perry and the people in Holcomb, leaving the reader longing to discover what happens on both perspectives of the story. More importantly, he ends many of the segments with surprising and suspenseful actions and thoughts. For example, when Nancy broaches her suspicions about the smell of cigarette smoke, Capote cunningly ends with this thought: "Before she could ask if this was really what Nancy meant, Nancy cut her off: 'Sorry, Susie. I've got to go. Mrs. Katz is here'" (22). This ending leaves the reader wondering whether Mr. Clutter, who possesses a strong aversion toward such matters, would actually take part in smoking. This suspected, sudden change in the daily habits of the family allows Capote to stir up a suspenseful atmosphere in the reader's mind because these details seem to foreshadow the murder. In addition, Capote amplifies the suspense by ending the section on this note, leaving the reader at a climactic point. Furthermore, as Capote switches back to the murderers, he describes their preparations in a casual manner. The tensions thus increases as the reader becomes upset at the lack of morals of the murderers and the total obliviousness of the Clutter family toward the upcoming events. The constant switching also serves another purpose by bringing the reader into the actual story as he or she tries to keep up with simultaneous events as they occur. Furthermore, Capote presents many of the unfolding events through the testimonies of various citizens, which gives more credibility to the story.

In addition to the timely shifts in the novel, Capote engenders suspense by waiting to disclose various details of the story, most importantly of the actual murders. Capote chooses to stop the description of the "score" just as the murderers approach the house: "Dick doused the headlights, slowed down, and stopped until his eyes were adjusted to the moon-illuminated night. Presently, the car crept forward" (57). After this passage, Capote skips straight to the discovery of the dead victims. Capote utilizes this very effective tactic of skipping ahead in order to build suspense. He surprises the reader and leaves him or her with the desire to continue in order to unearth the facts and details of that hideous night. In addition to building suspense, this method again places the reader in the eyes of the bemused Holcomb citizens, as they are equally clueless on the details surrounding the murders. Similarly, Capote does not explicitly introduce the murder plot: "Still no sign of Dick. But he was sure to show up; after all, the purpose of their meeting was Dick's idea, his 'score'" (14). Referring to the murder plot as the "score" serves various purposes. First, this reference adds to the suspenseful ambience because the reader cannot decipher its exact meaning; he or she can only construe that the term refers in some manner to the murder. Secondly, it puts the reader in the eyes and thoughts of Perry because he too appears incognizant of the actual plan before meeting Dick. Finally, during the period between the meeting and the murders, Capote adheres to using the reference "score" so that he may keep any motives and details mysterious and suspenseful. Again, Capote masterfully puts the reader into the eyes of the curious Holcomb citizens because neither the reader nor the citizens become aware of the motive until much later in the novel.

In addition to using suspense as an efficacious tool in retaining the reader's interest, Capote also brings into play an aspect of tension during the court trials and psychiatric evaluations. Capote commences to impose his own thoughts and beliefs into the story during the court trials. He lucidly demonstrates his condemnation of the M'Naghten Rule due to its tight strictures and inflexibility: "But had Dr. Jones been permitted to discourse on the cause of his indecision, he would have testified: 'Perry Smith shows definite signs of severe mental illness'" (296). By including the statements of Dr. Jones, if he would have been allowed to speak further, Capote evinces his concern and frustration over the utilization of the death penalty when dealing with the insane. A one word response to a question dealing with whether or not a person is insane is, of course, hardly sufficient to convey the full scope of the evaluation, especially if the subject's life depends on this evaluation. Capote also probes the inner mind of Perry Smith during his incarceration: "Eventually he wondered if perhaps he had invented them (a notion that he 'might not be normal, maybe insane' had troubled him 'even when I was little, and my sisters laughed because I liked moonlight. To hide in the shadows and watch the moon')" (265). This passage creates tension and the reader's mind vacillates on whether or not Perry experienced schizophrenia. Moreover, by including this passage, Capote foments a feeling of sympathy for the murderer. Throughout the beginning of the novel, the reader feels animosity towards Perry, but as Capote discloses these new details, the reader begins to reevaluate his or her previous convictions. Thus, Capote again allows the reader to see things through Perry's perspective. Once more, tension arises from a sudden shift in the mindset of the reader. Nonetheless, Capote leaves the reader with an ambiguous ending. Only the reader can decide whether Perry could acknowledge his actions as wrong on that horrific night or if the emotional and physical scars created by Perry's childhood drove him insane.

Thus, because Capote effectively uses tools of suspense and tension, he retains the reader's interest throughout the entire novel. The simultaneous shifting between events, delaying of crucial facts and details till later in the story, and the questioning of the court's laws on cases dealing with the insane and the death penalty are only some of the mechanisms Capote utilizes to conceive an extremely powerful and intriguing novel.

Essay: In Cold Blood: Retaining the Reader's Interest throu...

Essay: The Narrator's Perspective in True Crime Books

by Timothy Sexton
May 08, 2007

In Cold Blood, All the President's Men and Midnight in the Garden of Good of Evil all deal with real-life crimes. Each of the authors takes a different approach to point of view, depending upon their unique relationships to the setting in which the books take place. All three books, furthermore, combine certain elements of journalism and of the novel to create works that move beyond mere crime reporting to bring characters to life.

In 1959, the Clutter family was murdered in the small Kansas town of Holcomb. Soon thereafter, Truman Capote arrived to do research into the case for an article. Six years later, however, what Truman Capote produced was a revolutionary new book titled In Cold Blood. Capote's intention was to create a new literary genre that told a true story, but read like a novel. Thus, In Cold Blood reconstructs the gruesome murders of several members of the Clutter family, written more like a novel of realism than an example of a journalistic book like All the President's Men. Both books, however, deal primarily with a case of real murder. Yet Midnight in the Garden of Good and Evil differs substantially from the other two works, making a murder simply the central tile in a much larger mosaic.

Furthermore, much of the interest in Midnight is centred around place, not plot. Indeed, one might well suggest that the most important character in the book is not Jim Williams, but rather the city of Savannah, the description of which-"this is a town where gentlemen own their own white tie and tails"-is meant as a tribute to the distinctiveness of its citizens. The setting of In Cold Blood also is important, but the small Kansas town of Holcomb is portrayed as if it had not changed since the Depression. Where Berendt makes Savannah seem as peculiar as its residents, Capote is much more sentimental, using such imagery as "the well-loved piece of prairie where he had always hoped to build a house." Contrasting with both of these depictions of setting is Woodward and Bernstein's Washington, DC. As with the rest of the narrative style of this book, the nation's power center is presented straightforwardly, but with a sinister overtone: The shadows of its tall monuments and gleaming federal structures seem to contain unknown depths of suspicious activity.

Thus, the cities in which the crimes that these three books take place are important, to varying degrees, in determining the attitude of the authors. Each locale differs from one another in time and place. Capote's small Kansas farm town is almost the model of a taciturn community where nobody goes out of their way to appear unique; as a result Capote writes in a bare, stripped-down style. Berendt's Savannah is the exact opposite, a city that revels in its offbeat people, and his narrative, too, reflects that wide-open style. Meanwhile, Washington, D.C. is a city notorious for presenting a front that suggests strength and dependability, yet that hides colorful corruption taking place. Again, the author's style reflects that theme.

Thus, the time and locale of these books are important elements in determining how the narrators write their stories. Equally important, however, is the relationship of the authors to those settings. For instance, on the surface, Truman Capote appears to be one of the unlikeliest authors of the period to psychologically penetrate the minds of both the victims and killers in an isolated Midwest town. Capote was already famous not just for his writing, but for his flamboyantly homosexual lifestyle. He could not have been more removed from the humble townsfolk of Holcomb, or the sociopathic alienation of the killers. Before he became famous, however, Capote lived in a tiny southern hamlet that likely shared much in common with Holcomb; his connection doubtless gave him insight. Indeed, of the authors who wrote these three books, it is likely that Capote had the most ease in translating his vision to the general populace. Thus, Capote is quite successful in using small details that many readers could recognize in their own hometowns, such as his description of the abandoned building where the "Dance" sign no longer lit up. The simplicity of his description is also an indication of Capote's empathy for his characters. The Clutter family is presented as a mid-century American ideal, almost like something out of a sitcom. Capote paints Mr. Clutter, for example, as both a determined farmer and a respected citizen. His daughter comes across as the living embodiment of one of those characters by played Sandra Dee or Annette Funicello: "a straight-A student, the president of her class, a leader in the 4-H program and the Young Methodists League, a skilled rider, an excellent musician (piano, clarinet), an annual winner at the county fair (pastry, preserves, needlework, flower arrangement)..." (18). Only the fact that these people will be brutally murdered separates them from a thousand other families.

While Truman Capote came to Kansas from a small southern town by way of New York, John Berendt arrived in one of the iconic cities of old world southern gentility as nothing less than the traditional enemy: a Yankee from New York. Not only did he hail from New York, but he wrote for a magazine called the New Yorker. Nevertheless, he may have been fortunate in choosing Savannah as his southern city of choice: "We're famously hospitable, in fact, even by Southern standards. Savannah's called the 'Hostess City of the South,' you know." Nevertheless, it is specifically Berendt's status as an outsider that lends his book strength. Berendt's fame and charm gets him access to such Savannah staples as the Married Women's Club, the Black Debutantes' Ball, and Williams' legendary Christmas party. Berendt's mission differs substantially from both Capote's and Woodward and Bernstein's. The focus of those two books is the crime itself; how and why it happened in the former and learning exactly what happened in the latter. Berendt, in contrast, spends a considerable amount of time giving the reader a sense of place before the murder even occurs. The goal seems to be to introduce the elements that could conceivably lead to such a crime and the tortuous route to justice that follows. The suspected murderer in the book is himself something of a charming outsider, and it is possible that Berendt identifies most closely with Williams. Berendt clearly enjoys his cast of oddball characters, and the intent of the structure seems to be to create the feeling that in Savannah society, a scandal of this type is bound to happen. Thus, the book stands alongside All the President's Men, but in stark contrast to In Cold Blood, in terms of how the setting might inform--and even create--the crime.

Where Woodward and Bernstein differ from Berendt is in their attitudes toward the characters in their book, although the attitude is shaped by their relationship to the city. The attitude is also reflected in the surprising point of view that the two authors use. Each of these examinations into a crime are written using a different perspective. Capote attempts to impose omniscience into his narrative, describing not just the events, but also the thoughts of his characters. Berendt uses first-person narration, thus becoming another character in the vast panorama that is Savannah. Yet the most unique choice was made by Woodward and Bernstein. Since the two investigative reporters are the main characters it might have been expected they would use the first-person, perhaps with Woodward writing one chapter and Bernstein the next. Instead, they treat their book in the same way they wrote their newspaper articles. Although disconcerting at first to read the authors of the book referring to themselves in the third person and detached from analytic insight, eventually the purpose becomes clear. Writing in the third person better approximates journalistic objectivity and integrity. The reader is better able to make his own decisions about the techniques and tricks that reporters must use to get their story. The writing style is matter-of-fact and lends an authoritative weight that could be damaged by intrusions of the character' opinions. In addition, by distancing themselves from their own characters, Woodward and Bernstein transform into players within the larger drama rather than just reporting on it. This is important because the attitude that they take toward the people they are writing about is left entirely to the reader, including the attitude they have about themselves. All the President's Men ultimately is not a book about politics, therefore, but a book about journalism. As the two recent movies on the subject indicate, Truman Capote also could have injected himself into his narrative and turned In Cold Blood into more closely approximating the Watergate book. Equally true is that Woodward and Bernstein could have written their book using Capote's by utilizing all the copious notes they collected to attempt to get inside the head of those involved in the Watergate scandal. Instead, wisely, they chose the journalistic approach that reports only what can be verified. The result is that of the three books, All the President's Men is the one that invests the reader with the most responsibility for figuring out where the two authors stand.

Ultimately, any analysis of the narrator's attitude in a book about crime comes down to how the author feels about the criminal and each of these books take different routes. Clearly, the criminal in a book about crime, especially if he is convicted and proven guilty, will not come across as well as his victims. It is also true, however, that the criminal tends to be presented with more complexity than the victims. This could be due in part, when murder is involved, to the fact that the writer often does not have access into the mind of the victim. It is this very element that makes In Cold Blood the most controversial of the three books. There is no question that Capote utilized dramatic license in presenting the thoughts of the murderers. It may be easier to sympathize with them than it might have otherwise. It is quite obvious that Capote does not judge the two killers as harshly as one might expect. Whether or not one can say he actually likes them or not may be difficult, but there is certainly an attempt being made to present them as human beings instead of bloodthirsty animals. Although many readers may be repelled by this idea, it does serve the purpose of pointing out that killing them in effect renders the state somewhat inhumane.

Berendt takes an approach that is both different, and similar, to Capote's. Berendt's suspect is not an uneducated, lower-class drifter who committed multiple murders in cold blood, and that Joe Williams is a charming rich man makes all the difference. Whether or not Williams really did commit murder or not does not matter; fewer readers are likely to be repulsed that he is presented as a three-dimensional human being, than if they read Capote's portrayal of his murderers. Money makes a difference, and that is a subtext Berendt's books. For example, the expectation among many in Savannah was that Williams would get off simply because he had the money to do so. Yet precious few people thought Capote's murderous duo would not hang.

Woodward and Bernstein differ from both Capote and Berendt. Although they too get to know the participants personally and interact with them, they always manage to keep their objective distance. Whether describing the victims of Watergate or the known perpetrators, the two reporters insistently refrain from shaping the reader's opinions by introducing their own. In many ways, this makes All the President's Men the most effective of the books for the reader when it comes to shaping one's own attitude toward the participants.

Thus, In Cold Blood, All the President's Men and Midnight in the Garden of Good and Evil each undertake to describe the events surrounding a crime. Each book presents a different point of view that reflects how the time and place and events are impressed upon the author. In addition, the books stand as starkly different examples of how to treat the people who are involved in real life events. None of these books read like dry police reports, and although Capote's is the only one that fashions itself as a nonfiction novel, in reality, all three books possess the narrative drive and characterization that make a novel so interesting.

Quiz 1

1. **How many children do the Clutters have?**
   A. Six
   B. Two
   C. Four
   D. Three

2. **What is the supposed medical cause of Bonnie Clutter's depression?**
   A. Misplaced vertebrae
   B. Mental illness
   C. Nerve damage
   D. Hormonal imbalance

3. **Why won't Herb consider allowing Nancy to marry Bobby?**
   A. The Rupps are Catholic, and the Clutters are Methodist.
   B. He does not believe Bobby will be able to support Nancy.
   C. He doesn't like Bobby.
   D. Herb doesn't get along with Bobbyâ" s father.

4. **What does Nancy teach Jolene Katz to do?**
   A. Math problems
   B. Bake a cherry pie
   C. Play the trumpet
   D. Ride a horse

5. **Which of the following is NOT one of Nancy's activites?**
   A. Tennis
   B. Playing the clarinet
   C. Young Methodists' League
   D. Class office

6. **What is Dick's occupation?**
   A. Auto mechnanic
   B. Custodian
   C. Store clerk
   D. Car salesman

7. **What is to blame for the disfigurement of Dick's face?**
   A. A car accident
   B. A prison fight
   C. An accident with farming equipment
   D. He was born that way

8. **Who is Cookie?**
   A. A prostitute from Yokohama
   B. Perry's high school girlfriend
   C. A waitress Perry met in Honolulu
   D. Perry's nurse in the Washington State hospital

9. **Why has Kenyon been spending so much time alone?**
   A. He is depressed.
   B. His best friend has started "going with a girl."
   C. He has been busy with schoolwork.
   D. Herb has grounded him for smoking.

10. **For whom is Kenyon building the chest in the basement?**
    A. Nancy, whose birthday is next week
    B. Himself
    C. His parents, whose wedding anniversary is approaching
    D. His sister Beverly, who is getting married

11. **Who is Willie-Jay?**
    A. A Reverend who taught Perry about Christianity
    B. Perry's friend from the Kansas State Penitentiary, who called him "exceptional"
    C. Perry's oldest friend from childhood
    D. Perry's friend from Washington, who took care of him after his hospitalization

12. **Why does Perry originally return to Kansas City?**
    A. To reconnect with Willie-Jay
    B. To find his father
    C. To speak with Floyd Wells
    D. To meet with Reverend Post

13. **What is Herb Clutter's preferred mode of payment?**
    A. Credit
    B. Exchange of services
    C. Cash
    D. Check

14. **What is Perry's stage name in his fantasy about becoming a musician?**
    A. Perry-Jay Smith
    B. Perry the Great
    C. Perry O'Parsons
    D. Perry Porter

15. **Which of the following is NOT a place that Perry fantasizes about?**
    A. Mexico
    B. Australia
    C. Japan
    D. Sierra Madre

16. **Why is Teddy a poor guard dog?**
    A. He is too old and feeble to stand up to an intruder.
    B. He is blind.
    C. He is afraid of guns.
    D. He is too small to be intimidating.

17. **Why has Nancy stopped wearing Bobby's ring?**
    A. She learned that Bobby was drinking at a wedding he attended recently.
    B. She heard a rumor that Bobby was flirting with another girl.
    C. She is getting ready to break up with him.
    D. She is trying to deceive her father about how serious the relationship is.

18. **Why did Dick change his mind about Perry and decide to fold him in to his plans?**
    A. Perry earned the esteem of Willie-Jay, which Dick himself had been unable to do.
    B. Perry told him a story about killing a man in Las Vegas for kicks.
    C. Perry murdered another inmate at the Kansas State Penitentiary.
    D. Floyd Wells had vouched for Perry's abilities.

19. **What is Perry and Dick's excuse for leaving town overnight?**
    A. They are visiting Willie-Jay after his release from the penitentiary.
    B. They are visiting Dick's uncle in Kansas City.
    C. They are visiting Perry's sister in Fort Scott.
    D. They heard that temporary work might be available in Topeka.

20. **Why does Nancy Ewalt go to the Clutter home on Sunday morning?**
    A. To accompany the Clutters to church
    B. To have a trumpet lesson with Nancy Clutter
    C. To relay a message from Susan Kidwell
    D. To deliver the newspaper

21. **Where are the bodies of Mr. Clutter and Kenyon found?**
    A. In the backyard
    B. In the basement
    C. In their bedrooms
    D. In the living room

22. **How were the Clutters killed?**
    A. With a shotgun
    B. Strangulation
    C. Stabbing
    D. Poisoning

23. **Who becomes the initial suspect?**
    A. Paul Helm, the groundskeeper
    B. Vere English, Beverly Clutter's fiance
    C. Bobby Rupp
    D. Alfred Stoecklein, the hired man

24. **Where do Dick and Perry go immediately after committing the crimes?**
    A. Olathe
    B. Mexico
    C. Las Vegas
    D. Kansas City

25. **Which of the following is NOT stated as a reason that Alvin Dewey takes charge of the Clutter case?**

    A. He is one of the best and most experienced detectives at the K.B.I.

    B. He is hand-selected by Earl Robinson, the Finney county sheriff.

    C. He is more familiar with the happenings in Holcomb than anyone else at the K.B.I.

    D. He was a close personal friend of Herb and Bonnie Clutter.

Quiz 1 Answer Key

1. **(C)** Four
2. **(A)** Misplaced vertebrae
3. **(A)** The Rupps are Catholic, and the Clutters are Methodist.
4. **(B)** Bake a cherry pie
5. **(A)** Tennis
6. **(A)** Auto mechnanic
7. **(A)** A car accident
8. **(D)** Perry's nurse in the Washington State hospital
9. **(B)** His best friend has started "going with a girl."
10. **(D)** His sister Beverly, who is getting married
11. **(B)** Perry's friend from the Kansas State Penitentiary, who called him "exceptional"
12. **(A)** To reconnect with Willie-Jay
13. **(D)** Check
14. **(C)** Perry O'Parsons
15. **(B)** Australia
16. **(C)** He is afraid of guns.
17. **(A)** She learned that Bobby was drinking at a wedding he attended recently.
18. **(B)** Perry told him a story about killing a man in Las Vegas for kicks.
19. **(C)** They are visiting Perry's sister in Fort Scott.
20. **(A)** To accompany the Clutters to church
21. **(B)** In the basement
22. **(A)** With a shotgun
23. **(C)** Bobby Rupp
24. **(A)** Olathe
25. **(C)** He is more familiar with the happenings in Holcomb than anyone else at the K.B.I.

Quiz 2

1. **What is the primary piece of evidence found at the crime scene?**
   A. Fingerprints on Kenyon's hope chest
   B. There is no evidence found at the crime scene.
   C. Two pairs of boot tracks
   D. The 12-gauge shotgun

2. **Who calls the residents of Holcomb a "liver-lilied lot, shaking in their boots"?**
   A. Dick
   B. Alvin Dewey
   C. Myrtle Clare
   D. The narrator

3. **What does Perry's yellow parrot do in his dream?**
   A. Lead him to buried treasure
   B. Reunite him with his family
   C. Heal his injured legs
   D. Rescue him from tormentors

4. **What makes Dick momentarily regret passing the bogus checks?**
   A. He suddenly fears that he might get caught.
   B. He empathizes with the experience of being cheated out of money.
   C. He realizes that his parents will have to cover the charges.
   D. He realizes that stealing is a sin.

5. **Which of the following was NOT taken from the Clutter home on the night of the killings?**
   A. Forty-three dollars
   B. Kenyon's radio
   C. Nancy's wristwatch
   D. A pair of binoculars

6. **In his letter to the Telegram, what does Bonnie's brother urge the people of Garden City to do?**
   A. To come forward with information about the case
   B. To forgive and pray for the killers
   C. To seek the death penalty if the killers are apprehended
   D. To honor the memory of his sister and her family

7. **Who is Otto?**
    A. An intruder at the Clutter house who becomes a suspect
    B. A German lawyer whom Perry and Dick befriend in Acapulco
    C. An Austrian businessman who buys Kenyon's radio
    D. A detective from Kansas City who joins the investigation

8. **Why do Perry and Dick decide to return to the United States?**
    A. They are robbed in Mexico City.
    B. The wages in Mexico are too low.
    C. Dick hears about the possibility of another "score" in Kansas City.
    D. The Mexican police are collaborating on the murder investigation.

9. **Why did Perry move around so much as a child?**
    A. His father was a traveling salesman.
    B. His father was in the military.
    C. His parents were touring the Western rodeo circuit.
    D. His parents were trying to evade the IRS.

10. **What originally caused Perry's parents to separate?**
    A. Tex John left Flo for another woman.
    B. Tex John moved to Alaska, taking Perry with him.
    C. Flo took up drinking, and took the children with her to San Francisco.
    D. They disagreed over whether to put Perry in the Catholic orphanage.

11. **Why did the nuns at the Catholic orphanage beat Perry?**
    A. For trying to run away
    B. For telling them that he did not believe in God
    C. For wetting the bed
    D. For stealing

12. **How old was Perry when he enlisted in the Merchant Marine?**
    A. Sixteen
    B. Eighteen
    C. Twenty-one
    D. Twenty-three

13. **What was the cause of Perry's final row with this father?**
    A. Tex Joh scolded Perry for breaking parole.
    B. Tex John blamed Perry for the failure of the hunting lodge.
    C. Perry stole money from Tex John.
    D. Tex John made fun of Perry's yellow parrot dream.

14. **What happened to Fern?**
    A. She poisoned herself.
    B. She fell from a window.
    C. She disappeared.
    D. She died in a car accident.

15. **Which of the following is NOT a criticism that Barbara makes of Perry in her letter?**
    A. He looks down on Tex John for being undereducated.
    B. He has not made enough of an effort to stay in touch with her.
    C. He is too self-centered and antisocial.
    D. He is too quick to blame their parents for his own problems.

16. **How does Perry claim to feel about Barbara?**
    A. He loathes her.
    B. He tolerates her, but finds her irritating.
    C. He regrets that they don't see eye-to-eye.
    D. He misses her.

17. **Which of the following best captures Willie-Jay's "impression" of Barbara?**
    A. Superficial and flaky
    B. Nosy and condescending
    C. Narcissistic and aloof
    D. Narrow-minded and hypocritical

18. **Which of the following sums up Perry's view of life, according to his journal?**
    A. Good things come to those who wait.
    B. One shouldn't worry about things, because human life is insignificant.
    C. What goes around comes around.
    D. Life is cruel, and there's nothing anyone can do about it.

19. **Prior to arresting the killers, what does Alvin Dewey think the motive for the murders must have been?**
    A. All the other answers
    B. Thievery
    C. Psychopathic hatred of the Clutters
    D. Personal vendetta against Herb Clutter

20. **How do Dick and Perry plan to make their way across the countryside?**
    A. By stowing away on a freight train
    B. By driving a tractor trailer
    C. By murdering a motorist and stealing his car
    D. By joining a rodeo circuit

21. **How did Dick meet Floyd Wells?**
    A. Willie-Jay introduced them.
    B. They were cellmates at the penitentiary.
    C. Floyd assisted Dick on another "score."
    D. They worked at the same auto repair shop.

22. **Why didn't Dick go to college?**
    A. He served jail time instead.
    B. He wasn't a good enough student.
    C. He thought it would be more worthwhile to start working right after high school.
    D. He couldn't afford to.

23. **Why did Dick leave his first wife?**
    A. He was ashamed that he couldn't support her and their children.
    B. She threw him out for drinking.
    C. He was arrested for attempted robbery.
    D. Another woman claimed that he had gotten her pregnant.

24. **According to Dick's parents, what was unusual about his behavior on Sunday, November 15th?**
    A. He fell asleep during the basketball game.
    B. He picked a fight with his younger brother.
    C. He seemed more distracted than usual.
    D. He wasn't hungry for dinner.

25. **Which of the following is NOT among the items that Agent Nye finds in Perry's room at the Las Vegas boardinghouse?**
    A. A pillow from Honolulu
    B. Many bottles of aspirin
    C. A scrapbook filled with pictures of weightlifters
    D. A pair of boots matching the prints at the crime scene

Quiz 2 Answer Key

1. **(C)** Two pairs of boot tracks
2. **(C)** Myrtle Clare
3. **(D)** Rescue him from tormentors
4. **(C)** He realizes that his parents will have to cover the charges.
5. **(C)** Nancy's wristwatch
6. **(B)** To forgive and pray for the killers
7. **(B)** A German lawyer whom Perry and Dick befriend in Acapulco
8. **(B)** The wages in Mexico are too low.
9. **(C)** His parents were touring the Western rodeo circuit.
10. **(C)** Flo took up drinking, and took the children with her to San Francisco.
11. **(C)** For wetting the bed
12. **(A)** Sixteen
13. **(B)** Tex John blamed Perry for the failure of the hunting lodge.
14. **(B)** She fell from a window.
15. **(B)** He has not made enough of an effort to stay in touch with her.
16. **(A)** He loathes her.
17. **(D)** Narrow-minded and hypocritical
18. **(B)** One shouldn't worry about things, because human life is insignificant.
19. **(A)** All the other answers
20. **(C)** By murdering a motorist and stealing his car
21. **(B)** They were cellmates at the penitentiary.
22. **(D)** He couldn't afford to.
23. **(D)** Another woman claimed that he had gotten her pregnant.
24. **(A)** He fell asleep during the basketball game.
25. **(D)** A pair of boots matching the prints at the crime scene

Quiz 3

1. **Who or what is the Lone Wolf?**
    A. A nickname for Tex John
    B. Perry's brother
    C. A nickname for Willie-Jay
    D. Flo's father

2. **How does Barbara feel about Perry?**
    A. She thinks that deep down he is still the person she loved when they were young.
    B. She partly admires his independent attitude.
    C. She wishes he would try to make amends with her.
    D. She is afraid of him and the side of their family he represents.

3. **From where do Dick and Perry steal the 1956 Chevrolet in which they are eventually arrested?**
    A. Topeka
    B. Kansas City
    C. Tenville Junction
    D. Omaha

4. **How do the K.B.I. detectives learn that Perry and Dick are in Kansas City?**
    A. A Kansas City detective recognizes them from their mug shots.
    B. Dick's parents feel obligated to report his parole violation.
    C. Dick starts passing bad checks again.
    D. Floyd Wells, working for the police in exchange for a reduced prison sentence, tracks them down.

5. **Where do Dick and Perry spend Christmas, 1959?**
    A. Olathe
    B. Acapulco
    C. Miami Beach
    D. Tallahassee

6. **What is Perry's immediate reaction to Dick's attempt to woo the young girl on the beach?**
    A. He is shocked to discover this side of Dick.
    B. He is jealous that Dick's attention is focused elsewhere.
    C. He is disgusted by Dick's lack of self-control.
    D. He pretends not to notice.

7. **Where are Perry and Dick arrested?**
    A. Olathe
    B. Las Vegas
    C. Miami Beach
    D. Kansas City

8. **What are Dick and Perry doing right before their arrest?**
    A. Picking up their belongings at the post office, which they had shipped from Mexico
    B. Fixing up the stolen Chevrolet
    C. Paying a visit to Perry's boardinghouse
    D. Dropping bad checks

9. **What coincidence occurs at the time of the arrest to make the detectives' case airtight?**
    A. Perry and Dick have just been talking about Floyd Wells, and are overheard by the police.
    B. Perry and Dick have just picked up a package containing two pairs of boots, which match the prints at the crime scene.
    C. The detectives finally determine that Mr. Hickock's shotgun is the same one that was used to kill the Clutters.
    D. Perry and Dick have just picked up a package containing the hunting knife that was used to slit Herb Clutter's throat.

10. **How do the detectives know that Dick's alibi is a lie?**
    A. Perry has accidentally fed them the wrong version of the story.
    B. The gas station attendant has placed them in Garden City on the night of the 14th.
    C. The prostitutes that he names do not actually exist.
    D. Perry has no sister in Fort Scott.

11. **Why are the residents of Holcomb not entirely satisfied at the arrest of Dick and Perry?**
    A. They believe that others may have been involved.
    B. They dread having to relive the horror of the murders in the form of a trial.
    C. They are wary of the publicity that the trial will bring to the town.
    D. They are afraid that unsavory details will be revealed in the course of the trial.

12. **While in the Clutter house, what experience caused Perry to stop and reflect on the indignity of what they were doing?**
    A. Rooting around in Herb Clutter's billfold
    B. Kenyon's helpless expression as Perry was tying him up
    C. Crawling on his stomach to retrieve Nancy's silver dollar
    D. Bonnie's meek resignation

13. **How did Nancy Clutter act during the attempted robbery?**
    A. Irrational and panicky
    B. Cool-headed and composed
    C. Quiet and resigned
    D. Indignant and upset

14. **Which of the following experiences was NOT a source of frustration between Dick and Perry on the night of the shootings?**
    A. Perry put a stop to Dick's sexual conquest of Nancy.
    B. They disagreed over whether it was necessary to kill the Clutters.
    C. The safe they had expected to find did not exist.
    D. The Clutters were uncooperative.

15. **Which of the following best describes Perry's feelings right before he slits Mr. Clutter's throat?**
    A. Uncontrollable anger
    B. Hysterical fear
    C. Shame and self-pity
    D. Sadistic pleasure

16. **Which of the following is NOT stated as one of the reasons that Alvin Dewey is able to feel sympathy for Perry?**
    A. Perry's own life has been pitiable and fraught with misfortune.
    B. Though the murder was planned, the actual killings were carried out because Perry lost control of his emotions.
    C. Dewey feels that Dick was truly to blame for creating the psychological conditions that ignited Perry's rampage.
    D. The crime was not caused by a personal hatred of the Clutters.

17. **What is the crowd's reaction to the arrival of the killers in Garden City?**
    A. Jeering abusiveness
    B. Frustrated indignity
    C. Subdued silence
    D. Inconsolable anger

18. **On what day do the killers arrive in Garden City?**
    A. April 6, 1960
    B. January 1, 1960
    C. January 6, 1960
    D. January 6, 1961

19. **What is the Corner?**
    A. A nickname for Death Row
    B. A nickname for the jury box in a trial with a predictable outcome
    C. A blunt weapon carried by the county Sheriff
    D. A nickname for the gallows at the Kansas State Penitentiary

20. **Where is Perry's cell at the Garden City jailhouse located?**
    A. In a nearby annex
    B. Inside the Sheriff's residence
    C. Next to Dick's cell
    D. On the fourth floor

21. **Who is Josephine Meier?**
    A. One of the trial jurors
    B. A witness who testifies on Dick's behalf
    C. The wife of the undersheriff, who resides in the Sheriff's Residence
    D. A kindly resident of Garden City who visits Perry regularly

22. **What revision does Perry make to his confession while he is in Garden City?**
    A. He admits that he lied about Dick wanting to take advantage of Nancy Clutter, to make himself look better.
    B. He claims that they also killed the Clutters' dog, Teddy, and buried him in the yard.
    C. He says that he really meant to kill Herb Clutter, because Herb reminded him of his father.
    D. He admits that he was responsible for all four deaths.

23. **What does Dick tell his parents about how the crime was committed?**
    A. He finds it too difficult to face his father.
    B. He admits that he and Perry are equally to blame, even though Perry is the one who actually carried out the murders.
    C. He blames Perry for the murders and for entering the house with the intent to kill.
    D. He admits that the whole plan was his idea.

24. **Where did Perry meet Don Cullivan?**
    A. The Army
    B. The Kansas State Penitentiary
    C. The Merchant Marine
    D. Alaska

25. What religious denomination is Don Cullivan?
   A. Jewish
   B. Baptist
   C. Catholic
   D. Methodist

Quiz 3 Answer Key

1. **(A)** A nickname for Tex John
2. **(D)** She is afraid of him and the side of their family he represents.
3. **(C)** Tenville Junction
4. **(C)** Dick starts passing bad checks again.
5. **(C)** Miami Beach
6. **(C)** He is disgusted by Dick's lack of self-control.
7. **(B)** Las Vegas
8. **(A)** Picking up their belongings at the post office, which they had shipped from Mexico
9. **(B)** Perry and Dick have just picked up a package containing two pairs of boots, which match the prints at the crime scene.
10. **(D)** Perry has no sister in Fort Scott.
11. **(A)** They believe that others may have been involved.
12. **(C)** Crawling on his stomach to retrieve Nancy's silver dollar
13. **(B)** Cool-headed and composed
14. **(D)** The Clutters were uncooperative.
15. **(C)** Shame and self-pity
16. **(C)** Dewey feels that Dick was truly to blame for creating the psychological conditions that ignited Perry's rampage.
17. **(C)** Subdued silence
18. **(C)** January 6, 1960
19. **(D)** A nickname for the gallows at the Kansas State Penitentiary
20. **(B)** Inside the Sheriff's residence
21. **(C)** The wife of the undersheriff, who resides in the Sheriff's Residence
22. **(D)** He admits that he was responsible for all four deaths.
23. **(C)** He blames Perry for the murders and for entering the house with the intent to kill.
24. **(A)** The Army
25. **(C)** Catholic

Quiz 4

1. **What experience caused Don Cullivan to embrace religion?**
   A. A near-fatal car accident
   B. Hearing about Perry's involvement in the Clutter killings
   C. Fighting in the Korean War
   D. His brother's death from leukemia

2. **What does the M'Naghten rule stipulate?**
   A. That defendants are legally responsible for their actions if they have somehow planned them in advance
   B. That the murder of a minor is more condemnable than the murder of someone over 18
   C. That defendants are legally responsible for their actions if they are capable of judging right from wrong
   D. That a defendant can only plead insanity if he has been previously treated for mental illness

3. **According to the book, for how much is Babe sold at the Clutter auction?**
   A. Fifty dollars
   B. Seventy-five dollars
   C. Sixty-five dollars
   D. One hundred dollars

4. **How many of the jurors were personally acquainted with Herb Clutter?**
   A. Eleven
   B. Fourteen
   C. Ten
   D. Four

5. **When, according to Perry, did he first begin to have trouble with the law?**
   A. In Alaska with Tex John
   B. After his motorcycle accident
   C. At the Catholic orphanage
   D. While he was living with Flo and his siblings in San Francisco

6. **Why in particular does Perry resent his father?**
   A. He did not teach Perry to be a good enough huntsman.
   B. Tex John did not allow him to get a proper education.
   C. He did not visit Perry in the hospital after Perry's motorcycle accident.
   D. Perry feels he did not treat Flo fairly in her lifetime.

7. **In his essay for the trial, what does Dick reveal about his motivation for breaking into the Clutter house?**

    A. Dick's father had a grudge against Herb Clutter from decades ago.

    B. The "score" was partially intended to impress Perry.

    C. He wanted to sexually assault Nancy Clutter.

    D. Dick had briefly met Kenyon Clutter the previous winter, and the boy had made a disparaging comment about Dick.

8. **How does Dick feel about his compulsion to steal and his sexual interest in children?**

    A. He is completely emotionally detached from his actions.

    B. They have always been a part of his nature, but he has only recently begun to act on them.

    C. He takes a sadistic pleasure in hurting others in this way.

    D. They are impulses that he finds difficult to control.

9. **According to Mr, Hickock, what change occurred in Dick's behavior after car accident?**

    A. There was no discernible change in Dick's behavior after the accident.

    B. He became much more antagonistic and aggressive.

    C. He became much more sexually promiscuous.

    D. He began to steal and gamble for the first time.

10. **Who of the following is NOT called to testify during the trial?**

    A. Susan Kidwell

    B. Barbara Johnson

    C. Alvin Dewey

    D. Floyd Wells

11. **What does Floyd Wells receive in exchange for testifying against Perry and Dick?**

    A. Parole

    B. Both B and C

    C. The $1000 reward

    D. Neither B nor C

12. **Who breaks down in tears during the trial?**

    A. Susan Kidwell

    B. Beverly Clutter

    C. Mr. Hickock

    D. Mrs. Hickcock

13. **In his conversation with Don Cullivan, how does Perry claim to feel about the murders?**

   A. Regretful for the situation it has landed him in, but unbothered by the crime itself.

   B. Ashamed for his loss of control on that night, but unapologetic.

   C. Fearful that he has committed an unforgivable sin.

   D. Deeply remorseful for the suffering he inflicted on the family.

14. **What is Perry's attitude toward God and religion?**

   A. He has no use for either.

   B. He believes in God, but disdains organized religion.

   C. He accepts Don's message of God's love and forgiveness.

   D. He hesitates to make a definitive judgment, preferring to keep an open mind.

15. **What does Dr. Jones conclude about Dick's mental state?**

   A. He suffers from paranoid schizophrenia.

   B. His mind is perfectly sound.

   C. He has a severe character disorder, accompanied by signs of brain damage.

   D. He suffers from manic depression.

16. **Which of the following is NOT stated as a symptom of Dick's pathology?**

   A. The need to compensate for feelings of inferiority and sexual inadequacy

   B. Low self-esteem

   C. Lack of concern for others

   D. Inability to manage frustration

17. **What does Dr. Jones conclude about Perry's mental state?**

   A. He suffers from paranoid schizophrenia.

   B. His mind is perfectly sound.

   C. He has untreated brain damage from his motorcycle accident, but no definitive symptoms of mental illness.

   D. He suffers from bipolar disorder.

18. **Which of the following is NOT stated as a symptom of Perry's pathology?**

   A. Poorly controlled rage, triggered by feelings of being slighted by others

   B. Repressed sexuality

   C. Inability to distinguish between reality and fantasy, or his own mental projections

   D. Sensitivity to criticism

19. **Why is Dr. Jones not allowed to provide his full testimony during the trial?**
    A. The court upholds the M'Naghten rule.
    B. Perry and Dick's lawyers do not think it will help their case.
    C. The prosecution calls Dr. Jones's credentials into question.
    D. The court upholds the Durham rule.

20. **According to the article by Dr. Satten, which "key figure in a past traumatic configuration" did Mr. Clutter represent for Perry?**
    A. The nuns at the Catholic orphanage
    B. His father
    C. Any and all of the answers below
    D. The Army sergeant who was brutal to him

21. **What was Lowell Lee Andrews's crime?**
    A. Murdering his biology professor
    B. A shooting rampage at a local movie theater
    C. Rape and torture of an eighteen year-old girl
    D. Murdering his parents and sister

22. **What does the Durham rule stipulate?**
    A. The court is obligated to hear the testimony of a psychologist in the trial proceedings.
    B. Mental incompetence is not an acceptable defense in the case of premeditated murder.
    C. If mental incompetence played a role in the commission of a crime, the defendant is not responsible.
    D. If a defendant pleads insanity, he is entitled to a psychiatric evaluation.

23. **Who is "the journalist" referred to on page 335?**
    A. A biographer of Dick Hickock
    B. Truman Capote
    C. Harper Lee
    D. A reporter from the New York Times

24. **Who writes to the warden about Perry, prompting him to abandon his hunger strike?**
    A. Truman Capote
    B. Tex John
    C. Joe James
    D. Willie-Jay

25. **On what day are Perry and Dick hanged?**
     A. January 1st, 1965
     B. November 14th, 1965
     C. April 14th, 1963
     D. April 14th, 1965

Quiz 4 Answer Key

1. **(D)** His brother's death from leukemia
2. **(C)** That defendants are legally responsible for their actions if they are capable of judging right from wrong
3. **(B)** Seventy-five dollars
4. **(D)** Four
5. **(D)** While he was living with Flo and his siblings in San Francisco
6. **(B)** Tex John did not allow him to get a proper education.
7. **(C)** He wanted to sexually assault Nancy Clutter.
8. **(D)** They are impulses that he finds difficult to control.
9. **(D)** He began to steal and gamble for the first time.
10. **(B)** Barbara Johnson
11. **(B)** Both B and C
12. **(D)** Mrs. Hickcock
13. **(A)** Regretful for the situation it has landed him in, but unbothered by the crime itself.
14. **(A)** He has no use for either.
15. **(C)** He has a severe character disorder, accompanied by signs of brain damage.
16. **(C)** Lack of concern for others
17. **(A)** He suffers from paranoid schizophrenia.
18. **(B)** Repressed sexuality
19. **(A)** The court upholds the M'Naghten rule.
20. **(C)** Any and all of the answers below
21. **(D)** Murdering his parents and sister
22. **(C)** If mental incompetence played a role in the commission of a crime, the defendant is not responsible.
23. **(B)** Truman Capote
24. **(B)** Tex John
25. **(D)** April 14th, 1965

Quiz 5

1. **What does Perry do in his last moments before his death?**
    A. Attempt to take his own life
    B. Dream of the yellow bird
    C. Apologize for the crime
    D. Ask for God's forgiveness

Quiz 5 Answer Key

    1. **(C)** Apologize for the crime

ClassicNotes

GradeSaver™

Getting you the grade since 1999™

Other ClassicNotes from GradeSaver™

12 Angry Men	Aristotle's Politics	Breakfast at Tiffany's
1984	Aristotle: Nicomachean	Breakfast of Champions
A&P and Other Stories	Ethics	The Brief Wondrous Life
Absalom, Absalom	As I Lay Dying	of Oscar Wao
Adam Bede	As You Like It	The Brothers Karamazov
The Adventures of Augie	Astrophil and Stella	The Burning Plain and
March	Atlas Shrugged	Other Stories
The Adventures of	Atonement	A Burnt-Out Case
Huckleberry Finn	The Awakening	By Night in Chile
The Adventures of Tom	Babbitt	Call of the Wild
Sawyer	The Bacchae	Candide
The Aeneid	Bartleby the Scrivener	The Canterbury Tales
Agamemnon	The Bean Trees	Cat on a Hot Tin Roof
The Age of Innocence	The Bell Jar	Cat's Cradle
The Alchemist (Coelho)	Beloved	Catch-22
The Alchemist (Jonson)	Benito Cereno	The Catcher in the Rye
Alice in Wonderland	Beowulf	Cathedral
All My Sons	Bhagavad-Gita	The Caucasian Chalk
All Quiet on the Western	Billy Budd	Circle
Front	Black Boy	Charlotte Temple
All the King's Men	Bleak House	Charlotte's Web
All the Pretty Horses	Bless Me, Ultima	The Cherry Orchard
Allen Ginsberg's Poetry	Blindness	The Chocolate War
The Ambassadors	Blood Meridian: Or the	The Chosen
American Beauty	Evening Redness in	A Christmas Carol
The Analects of	the West	Christopher Marlowe's
Confucius	Blood Wedding	Poems
And Then There Were	The Bloody Chamber	Chronicle of a Death
None	Bluest Eye	Foretold
Angela's Ashes	The Bonfire of the	Civil Disobedience
Animal Farm	Vanities	Civilization and Its
Anna Karenina	The Book of Daniel	Discontents
Anthem	The Book of the Duchess	A Clockwork Orange
Antigone	and Other Poems	Coleridge's Poems
Antony and Cleopatra	The Book Thief	The Color of Water
Aristotle's Poetics	Brave New World	The Color Purple

For our full list of over 250 Study Guides, Quizzes,
Sample College Application Essays, Literature Essays and E-texts, visit:

www.gradesaver.com

ClassicNotes

GrdeSaver™

Getting you the grade since 1999™

Other ClassicNotes from GradeSaver™

Comedy of Errors
Communist Manifesto
A Confederacy of
  Dunces
Confessions
Confessions of an
  English Opium Eater
Connecticut Yankee in
  King Arthur's Court
The Consolation of
  Philosophy
Coriolanus
The Count of Monte
  Cristo
The Country Wife
Crime and Punishment
The Crucible
Cry, the Beloved
  Country
The Crying of Lot 49
The Curious Incident of
  the Dog in the
  Night-time
Cymbeline
Daisy Miller
David Copperfield
Death in Venice
Death of a Salesman
The Death of Ivan Ilych
Democracy in America
Devil in a Blue Dress
Dharma Bums
The Diary of a Young
  Girl by Anne Frank
Disgrace

Divine Comedy-I:
  Inferno
Do Androids Dream of
  Electric Sheep?
Doctor Faustus
  (Marlowe)
A Doll's House
Don Quixote Book I
Don Quixote Book II
John Donne: Poems
Dora: An Analysis of a
  Case of Hysteria
Dr. Jekyll and Mr. Hyde
Dracula
Dubliners
The Duchess of Malfi
East of Eden
Electra by Sophocles
The Electric Kool-Aid
  Acid Test
Emily Dickinson's
  Collected Poems
Emma
Ender's Game
Endgame
Enduring Love
The English Patient
The Epic of Gilgamesh
Ethan Frome
The Eumenides
Everyman: Morality Play
Everything is Illuminated
Exeter Book
The Faerie Queene
Fahrenheit 451

The Fall of the House of
  Usher
A Farewell to Arms
The Federalist Papers
Fences
Fight Club
Fight Club (Film)
Flags of Our Fathers
Flannery O'Connor's
  Stories
For Whom the Bell Tolls
The Fountainhead
Frankenstein
Franny and Zooey
The Giver
The Glass Castle
The Glass Menagerie
The God of Small Things
Goethe's Faust
The Good Earth
The Good Woman of
  Setzuan
The Grapes of Wrath
Great Expectations
The Great Gatsby
Grendel
The Guest
Gulliver's Travels
Hamlet
The Handmaid's Tale
Hard Times
Haroun and the Sea of
  Stories
Harry Potter and the
  Philosopher's Stone
Heart of Darkness

For our full list of over 250 Study Guides, Quizzes,
Sample College Application Essays, Literature Essays and E-texts, visit:

www.gradesaver.com

ClassicNotes

GrﾑdeSaver™

Getting you the grade since 1999™

Other ClassicNotes from GradeSaver™

Hedda Gabler
Henry IV (Pirandello)
Henry IV Part 1
Henry IV Part 2
Henry V
Herzog
Hippolytus
The History of Tom
   Jones, a Foundling
The Hobbit
Homo Faber
The House of Bernarda
   Alba
House of Mirth
The House of the Seven
   Gables
The House of the Spirits
House on Mango Street
How the Garcia Girls
   Lost Their Accents
Howards End
A Hunger Artist
The Hunger Games
I Know Why the Caged
   Bird Sings
I, Claudius
An Ideal Husband
Iliad
The Importance of Being
   Earnest
In Cold Blood
In Our Time
In the Skin of a Lion
In the Time of the
   Butterflies
Inherit the Wind

An Inspector Calls
The Interesting Narrative
   of the Life of Olaudah
   Equiano
Interpreter of Maladies
Into the Wild
Invisible Man
The Island of Dr. Moreau
Jane Eyre
Jazz
The Jew of Malta
Johnny Tremain
Joseph Andrews
A Journal of the Plague
   Year
The Joy Luck Club
Jude the Obscure
Julius Caesar
The Jungle
Jungle of Cities
Kama Sutra
Kate Chopin's Short
   Stories
Kidnapped
King Lear
King Solomon's Mines
The Kite Runner
The Lais of Marie de
   France
Last of the Mohicans
Leaves of Grass
The Legend of Sleepy
   Hollow
A Lesson Before Dying
Leviathan
Libation Bearers

Life is Beautiful
Life of Pi
Light In August
Like Water for Chocolate
The Lion, the Witch and
   the Wardrobe
Little Women
Lolita
Long Day's Journey Into
   Night
A Long Way Gone
Look Back in Anger
Lord Byron's Poems
Lord Jim
Lord of the Flies
The Lord of the Rings:
   The Fellowship of the
   Ring
The Lord of the Rings:
   The Return of the
   King
The Lord of the Rings:
   The Two Towers
A Lost Lady
The Lottery and Other
   Stories
Love in the Time of
   Cholera
The Love Song of J.
   Alfred Prufrock
The Lovely Bones
Lucy
Macbeth
Madame Bovary
Maestro

For our full list of over 250 Study Guides, Quizzes,
Sample College Application Essays, Literature Essays and E-texts, visit:

www.gradesaver.com

ClassicNotes

GradeSaver™

Getting you the grade since 1999™

Other ClassicNotes from GradeSaver™

Maggie: A Girl of the Streets and Other Stories
Manhattan Transfer
Mankind: Medieval Morality Plays
Mansfield Park
The Marrow of Tradition
The Master and Margarita
MAUS
The Mayor of Casterbridge
Measure for Measure
Medea
Merchant of Venice
Metamorphoses
The Metamorphosis
Middlemarch
A Midsummer Night's Dream
The Mill on the Floss
Moby Dick
A Modest Proposal and Other Satires
Moll Flanders
The Most Dangerous Game
Mother Courage and Her Children
Mrs. Dalloway
Much Ado About Nothing
My Antonia
Mythology
The Namesake

Narrative of the Life of Frederick Douglass, An American Slave: Written by Himself
Native Son
Nervous Conditions
Never Let Me Go
Nickel and Dimed: On (Not) Getting By in America
Night
Nine Stories
No Exit
Northanger Abbey
Notes from Underground
O Pioneers
The Odyssey
Oedipus Rex or Oedipus the King
Of Mice and Men
The Old Man and the Sea
Oliver Twist
On Liberty
On the Road
One Day in the Life of Ivan Denisovich
One Flew Over the Cuckoo's Nest
One Hundred Years of Solitude
Oroonoko
Oryx and Crake
Othello
Our Town
The Outsiders
Pale Fire

Pamela: Or Virtue Rewarded
Paradise Lost
A Passage to India
The Pearl
Percy Shelley: Poems
Perfume: The Story of a Murderer
Persepolis: The Story of a Childhood
Persuasion
Phaedra
Phaedrus
The Piano Lesson
The Picture of Dorian Gray
Pilgrim's Progress
Poe's Poetry
Poe's Short Stories
Poems of W.B. Yeats: The Rose
Poems of W.B. Yeats: The Tower
The Poems of William Blake
The Poisonwood Bible
Pope's Poems and Prose
Portrait of the Artist as a Young Man
The Praise of Folly
Pride and Prejudice
The Prince
The Professor's House
Prometheus Bound
Pudd'nhead Wilson
Purple Hibiscus

For our full list of over 250 Study Guides, Quizzes,
Sample College Application Essays, Literature Essays and E-texts, visit:

www.gradesaver.com

ClassicNotes

GradeSaver™

Getting you the grade since 1999™

Other ClassicNotes from GradeSaver™

Pygmalion
Rabbit, Run
A Raisin in the Sun
The Real Life of
  Sebastian Knight
Rebecca
The Red Badge of
  Courage
The Remains of the Day
The Republic
Rhinoceros
Richard II
Richard III
The Rime of the Ancient
  Mariner
Rip Van Winkle and
  Other Stories
The Road
Robert Browning: Poems
Robert Frost: Poems
Robinson Crusoe
Roll of Thunder, Hear
  My Cry
Romeo and Juliet
A Room of One's Own
A Room With a View
A Rose For Emily and
  Other Short Stories
Rosencrantz and
  Guildenstern Are
  Dead
Salome
The Scarlet Letter
The Scarlet Pimpernel
The Seagull

Season of Migration to
  the North
Second Treatise of
  Government
The Secret Life of Bees
The Secret River
Secret Sharer
Sense and Sensibility
A Separate Peace
Shakespeare's Sonnets
Shantaram
She Stoops to Conquer
Short Stories of Ernest
  Hemingway
Short Stories of F. Scott
  Fitzgerald
Siddhartha
Silas Marner
Sir Gawain and the
  Green Knight
Sir Thomas Wyatt:
  Poems
Sister Carrie
Six Characters in Search
  of an Author
Slaughterhouse Five
Snow Falling on Cedars
The Social Contract
Something Wicked This
  Way Comes
Song of Roland
Song of Solomon
Songs of Innocence and
  of Experience
Sons and Lovers

The Sorrows of Young
  Werther
The Sound and the Fury
The Sound of Waves
The Spanish Tragedy
Speak
Spenser's Amoretti and
  Epithalamion
Spring Awakening
The Stranger
A Streetcar Named
  Desire
A Study in Scarlet
Sula
The Sun Also Rises
Sundiata: An Epic of Old
  Mali
Tale of Two Cities
The Taming of the Shrew
The Tempest
Tender is the Night
Tess of the D'Urbervilles
Their Eyes Were
  Watching God
Things Fall Apart
The Things They Carried
A Thousand Splendid
  Suns
The Threepenny Opera
Through the Looking
  Glass
Thus Spoke Zarathustra
The Time Machine
Titus Andronicus
To Build a Fire
To Kill a Mockingbird

For our full list of over 250 Study Guides, Quizzes,
Sample College Application Essays, Literature Essays and E-texts, visit:

www.gradesaver.com

ClassicNotes

GradeSaver™

Getting you the grade since 1999™

Other ClassicNotes from GradeSaver™

To the Lighthouse
The Tortilla Curtain
Touching Spirit Bear
Treasure Island
Trifles
Troilus and Cressida
Tropic of Cancer
Tropic of Capricorn
Tuesdays With Morrie
The Turn of the Screw
Twelfth Night
Twilight
Ulysses
Uncle Tom's Cabin
Utopia
Vanity Fair
A Very Old Man With
    Enormous Wings
Villette
A Vindication of the
    Rights of Woman
The Visit
Volpone
Waiting for Godot
Waiting for Lefty
Walden
War and Peace
The Wars
Washington Square
The Waste Land
The Wave
The Wealth of Nations
Where the Red Fern
    Grows
White Fang

A White Heron and
    Other Stories
White Noise
White Teeth
Who's Afraid of Virginia
    Woolf
Wide Sargasso Sea
Wieland
Winesburg, Ohio
The Winter's Tale
The Woman Warrior
Wordsworth's Poetical
    Works
Woyzeck
A Wrinkle in Time
Wuthering Heights
The Yellow Wallpaper
Yonnondio: From the
    Thirties
Young Goodman Brown
    and Other Hawthorne
    Short Stories
Zeitoun

For our full list of over 250 Study Guides, Quizzes,
Sample College Application Essays, Literature Essays and E-texts, visit:

www.gradesaver.com

80929174R00066

Made in the USA
Lexington, KY
08 February 2018